Anti-Dumping

Global Abuse of a Trade Policy Instrument

PUBLISHED BY ACADEMIC FOUNDATION
IN ASSOCIATION WITH

LIBERTY

Liberty Institute
New Delhi

Read more about Liberty Institute
on the last page of this book

THE EDITORS

Bibek Debroy is Secretary General, PHD Chamber of Commerce and Industry, New Delhi. He is a professional economist and was educated in Presidency College (Calcutta), Delhi School of Economics and Trinity College (Cambridge). He has worked at Presidency College (Calcutta), Gokhale Institute of Politics and Economics (Pune), Indian Institute of Foreign Trade (Delhi), National Council of Applied Economic Research (Delhi) and as Consultant, Department of Economic Affairs, Ministry of Finance, Government of India. He has been the Director of the Rajiv Gandhi Institute for Contemporary Studies (RGICS), Rajiv Gandhi Foundation, New Delhi. He was also the Director for a project known as LARGE, set up by the Ministry of Finance and UNDP to examine legal reforms. He is the author and editor of several books, papers and popular articles and has been consulting editor and columnist with Business Standard. Bibek Debroy's special interests are international trade (in particular the WTO), law reform and the political economy of liberalisation in India. He has been listed in many bibliographies and has been a member of several government committees.

Debashis Chakraborty is Assistant Professor at the Indian Institute of Foreign Trade, New Delhi. Debashis has been educated at University of Calcutta and Centre for International Trade and Development, JNU. He has worked on issues pertaining to international trade policy, WTO issues and Indian economic development, and presented and published his research at various academic and policy forums in India and abroad. He has earlier worked in Rajiv Gandhi Institute for Contemporary Studies (RGICS), New Delhi as a researcher. Debashis has recently edited two titles on WTO and is currently working on a manuscript relating to Contract Farming in India.

Anti-Dumping

Global Abuse of a Trade Policy Instrument

Editors:

Bibek Debroy

Debashis Chakraborty

ACADEMIC FOUNDATION
NEW DELHI

First published in 2007
by :

ACADEMIC FOUNDATION
4772-73 / 23 Bharat Ram Road, (23 Ansari Road),
Darya Ganj, New Delhi - 110 002 (India).
Phones : 23245001 / 02 / 03 / 04.
Fax : +91-11-23245005.
E-mail : academic@vsnl.com
www. academicfoundation.com

in association with :

Liberty Institute, New Delhi
www.libertyindia.org

Anti-Dumping:
Global Abuse of a Trade Policy Instrument
editors: Bibek Debroy and Debashis Chakraborty

ISBN 10: 81-7188-589-6
ISBN 13: 978-81-7188-589-6

Typeset by Italics India, New Delhi.
Printed and bound in India.

Contents

List of Tables, Figures and Annexes

TABLES

FIGURES

ANNEXURES

Acronyms

AB	Appellate Body
AD	Anti-Dumping
ADA	Anti-Dumping Agreement
ADD	Anti-Dumping Duties
ASTAC	Ad Hoc Shrimp Trade Action Committee
ATC	Agreement on Textiles and Clothing
BTT	Board of Tariffs and Trade (South Africa)
CADP	Committee on Anti-Dumping Practices
CAG	Committee on Agriculture
CASS	Anti-Dumping and Subsidies Commission (Venezuela)
CESTAT	Customs, Excise & Service Tax Appellate (India)
CIF	Cost, Insurance, and Freight
CN	Combined Nomenclature
CV	Constructed Value
DA	Designated Authority
DC	Developing Country
DDA	Doha Development Agenda
DGAD	Directorate General of Anti-Dumping and Allied Duties (India)
DoC	Department of Commerce (US) (Same as US DoC)
DSB	Dispute Settlement Body
DSU	Dispute Settlement Understanding
EC	European Community

EM	Export Market
ESCAP	Economic and Social Commission for Asia and the Pacific
EU	European Union
FA	Facts Available
FDI	Foreign Direct Investment
GATT	General Agreement on Tariffs and Trade
GDP	Gross Domestic Product
HM	Home Market
HMP	Home Market Price
IDC	Industrial Development Corporation
IMF	International Monetary Fund
ITC	International Trade Commission (US) (Same as USITC)
LPUCI	Legislation on Prevention of Unfair Competition in Importation (Turkey)
MFN	Most Favoured Nation
MNEs	Multinational Enterprises
MTN	Multilateral Trade Negotiation
NICs	Newly-Industrialising Countries
NIEs	Newly-Industrialising Economies
NME	Non-Market Economy(ies)
NTB	Non-Tariff Barrier(s)
OECD	Organisation of Economic Cooperation and Development
PRC	People's Republic of China
QRs	Quantitative Restrictions
SCM	Subsidy and Countervailing Measures
SDT	Special and Differential Treatment
SEAI	Seafoods Exporters Association of India
SSIs	Small Scale Industries

TMP	Third Market Price
TRIPS	Trade-Related Aspects of Intellectual Property Rights
UN COMTRADE	United Nations Commodity Trade Statistics Database
UNCTAD	United Nations Conference of Trade and Development
US	United States
VAT	Value Added Tax
WTO	World Trade Organization

Contributors

Cengiz Bahçekapili ...... *Assistant Professor, Department of Economics, Marmara University, Bahçelievler-Istanbul, Turkey.*

Debashis Chakraborty .... *Assistant Professor, Indian Institute of Foreign Trade, New Delhi.*

Murat Çokgezen .... *Associate Professor, Department of Economics, Marmara University, Bahçelievler-Istanbul, Turkey.*

Bibek Debroy .... *Secretary General, PHD Chamber of Commerce and Industry, New Delhi.*

Fredrik Erixon .... *Chief Economist, Swedish Think Tank Timbro, Stockholm.*

Daniel Ikenson .... *Associate Director, Center for Trade Policy Studies, Cato Institute, Washington DC.*

Kofi Oteng Kufuor ...... *Reader, School of Law, University of East London, London.*

Yuefen Li .... *Senior Economic Affairs Officer in the Division on Globalization and Development Strategies at UNCTAD, Geneva and Guest Professor at Tsinghua University, China.*

Brink Lindsey .... *Vice President for Research, Cato Institute, Washington DC and a Contributing Editor at Reason magazine.*

K.D. Raju .... *Deputy Secretary, PHD Chamber of Commerce and Industry, New Delhi.*

Nicola Theron .... *Co-founder and the Managing Director, Econex, Cape Town and a Senior Lecturer at the Department of Economics, University of Stellenbosch, South Africa.*

Introduction

BIBEK DEBROY and DEBASHIS CHAKRABORTY

Dumping: Procedures and Implications

While the broad objective of the GATT/WTO framework is to facilitate global free trade, plenty of exemptions (e.g. anti dumping) to free trade principles are embedded in the agreement. The market access barriers caused through these avenues have always been and are becoming increasingly important tool for protectionist purposes, especially after the WTO-induced tariff reform taking place over the last decade. Therefore, strictly speaking, it is a myth that the GATT/WTO system talks only about free trade.

According to the GATT/WTO agreement, dumping is defined as exporting a product at lower than its 'normal value', while normal value is defined as the price, "in the ordinary course of trade, for the like product when destined for consumption in the exporting country." The definition implies that the normal value is accepted as a fair selling price in the domestic market of the exporting country, provided that the exported product is similar to (like product) the one sold in the domestic market. If however no like product is sold in the domestic market, or if the volume of these sales is insignificant, two alternative procedures can be applied for determining normal value. The first option is to compare the export price of the product in question with the export price of a like product to a third country. If however there are no such reasonable export prices available for comparison, a second option is to construct normal value on the basis of the cost of production in the country of origin, with mark-ups for administrative, selling and general costs and profits. The calculation of normal value through either of these methods may or may not prove the existence of dumping. However, the point to note is, dumping *per se* is not GATT/WTO incompatible; it is an offense only when a causal link between the act of dumping by the exporting country and the injury to the domestic industry in the importing country is established. Only when this link is established, anti-dumping procedure can be initiated.

To initiate an anti-dumping investigation, there has to be a written complaint on behalf of domestic industry, supported by a significant share of domestic producers. There are two complementary criteria to define 'significant'. One, the application must be supported by producers who account for at least 50 per cent of the total output and two, producers supporting the complaint must account for at least 25 per cent of output produced by producers who are not indifferent to the issue. Any unsubstantiated complaints are to be rejected. Investigation will also be terminated if the margin of dumping is found to be minimum or *de minimis*, defined as less than 2 per cent, expressed as a percentage of the export price, or, if the volume of dumped imports from any country accounts for less than 3 per cent market share of imports of the like product in the importing country, unless such exports collectively account for more than 7 per cent of the total imports. To restrict the misuse of anti-dumping duty (ADD), there is also a sunset clause available. Unless revalidated through a 'fresh' review, any ADD will expire after five years from the date of imposition. In other words, continuation of ADD indefinitely is not allowed. However, it is observed that various countries through back-to-back investigations bypass this provision and continue to impose ADD for some products for well beyond five years.

The fact that dumping *per se* is not GATT/WTO incompatible can ethically be supported by arguing that it should not be objectionable unless linked up with predatory policies and anti-trust legislation. For instance, market structures in the domestic market might be monopolistic or oligopolistic, permitting cross-subsidisation of exports. But this underlines entry barriers and distortions that allow such market structures to continue. Alternatively, government policies and non-transparent pricing might permit cross-subsidisation of exports. The issue basically needs to be tackled through competition policy, which will eventually come on WTO's agenda. Globally, if one looks at competition policies, they are based on structure (market shares), conduct (unfair or restrictive trade practices) or performance (price, profitability). Cross-country experiences also suggest that competition policies based on performance rarely work. Nor do competition policies based on structure, unless they involve demonopolisation of public sector monopolies or mergers and acquisitions. Successful competition policies are based on conduct. There exists a parallel there. The Anti-Dumping Agreement (ADA) has no link with conduct, but is based on prices alone. Therefore, it often taxes efficiency and subsidises inefficiency. If a cross-national competition policy agreement can be worked out through the WTO, the ADA should cease to have any further relevance. However, in the absence of ADA (Article VI), member countries will have the freedom to adopt whatever rules they wish on anti-dumping and such unilateral action is undesirable. Instead, Article VI needs to be disciplined and linked up to tests for predatory intent through competition policy provisions. Of course, there are and will be problems in implementation. Rare is the case when predatory intent can be demonstrated *a priori*. Established *post facto*, the harm has been done.

However, on the other hand the ADA is violative of basic free trade principles preached by GATT/WTO and needs to be scrapped from that standpoint. It is observed in the recent period that developed countries have lost comparative advantage in manufacturing sector and have become more protectionist. Conversely, developing countries stand to benefit from greater liberalisation and opening up. For instance, while for a developing country like India import-competing industries tend to lose if anti-dumping action is waived, welfare gains by the users (consumers and exporters) will be more than proportionate. On the other hand, Indian exporters will benefit from removal of NTBs that anti-dumping investigations amount to in the developed country markets. This is a reason why developing countries should ultimately argue for scrapping of the ADA. Even if the ADA is scrapped, within the GATT/WTO framework, temporary protection to domestic industry against injury is possible through the safeguards agreement, although unlike the ADA, use of the safeguards clause requires compensation to trading partners.

Negotiation on Anti-Dumping and the Concern Areas

The origins of anti-dumping legislation can be traced back to the 19th century, when the European sugar industries appealed to their respective governments for protection citing instances for dumping of imported sugar at unfairly low prices. It was observed during the mid-1890s that British steel industry suffered by low-priced German and American steel products across a broad product range in both overseas and domestic markets, which is sometimes argued as evidence of dumping.[1] In 1902, there was a formal agreement on anti-dumping. Canada was the first country to adopt the anti-dumping law in 1904 (there was an earlier version in the last decade of the 19th century), subsequently followed by other European countries and then the United States in 1916.[2]

The General Agreement on Tariffs and Trade (GATT) was set up in 1947 for liberalising world trade through a series of multilateral trade negotiation (MTN) rounds. The US law, modified in 1921, and the Canadian law, together formed the basis for the original GATT article (Article VI) on anti-dumping in 1947.[3] Subsequently, discussions on anti-dumping related issues during the Kennedy Round (1962-1967) and Tokyo Round (1973-1979) of MTNs helped the GATT members to arrive at several codes on this issue. For instance, the Tokyo Round code (effective from 1 January 1980 onwards) elaborated on Article VI, specifying the basis for imposition, collection and duration of ADD and allowing for negotiated agreements, known as *price undertakings*, between relevant parties. However the codes developed during Kennedy and Tokyo Round were plurilateral agreements, not multilateral ones and therefore were not binding on all GATT members. Only the interested countries were to be signatories in these provisions.

The Uruguay Round (1986-1994) ADA, being a multilateral agreement (i.e. binding on all GATT or WTO members) is a definite improvement over the Kennedy and Tokyo Round codes, especially on injury and establishing the causal link between dumping and injury.[4] Despite this improvement, misuses are however quite common owing to the several loopholes present in the agreement. First, the arbitrariness in determining 'like' product is a major grey area. If an exported product is not identical to a product sold in the domestic market, the alternate determination mechanism requires case-by-case cost-based adjustments to the sales price in the domestic market,

1. Thomas R. Howell and Dewey Ballantine, "Dumping: Still a Problem in International Trade", available at *http://www.dbtrade.com/publications/howell.pdf*.
2. This had a clause that predatory intent should exist. However, the GATT/WTO anti-dumping agreement requires no such proof of predatory intent to drive out competition.
3. Article VI stated, "the contracting parties recognise that dumping, by which products of one country are introduced into the commerce of another country at less than the normal value of the products, is to be condemned if it causes or threatens material injury to an established industry in the territory of a contracting party or materially retards the establishment of a domestic industry."
4. The WTO's website has a synopsis of the anti-dumping agreement and highlights its plus points.

which leaves enough scope for further arbitrariness. Second, the domestic sales price can be considered for the analysis if it is 'in the ordinary course of trade'. Thus, low prices charged for sales in the domestic market can be ignored on grounds of these not being arm's length transactions and, therefore, not in the ordinary course of trade. Alternatively, it can be argued that such sales price is below per unit average cost of production and should be disregarded. This often results in an overvaluation of domestic sales price, making it easier to prove the existence of dumping. Third, construction of the normal value involves complicated cost calculations and allocations (e.g. between sales in the domestic market and the export market). If there is a conflict between accounting practices in the exporting country and the importing country, investigating authorities typically follow accounting practices in the importing country. Sometimes, inappropriate accounting practices coupled with inefficient and non-transparent indirect tax structure makes it difficult to allocate costs appropriately. If such account books are not available, normal value can be constructed on the basis of the cost structure for the same general category of products for other exporters or producers or 'any other reasonable method'. GATT/WTO legitimise this by saying that if required information on costs is not available from exporters, investigations can be undertaken on the basis of 'best information', which can lead to further scope for arbitrariness. Fourth, comparison of the export price and sales price in the domestic market requires exchange rate conversions, and exchange rate fluctuations can significantly influence the comparison. The agreement stipulates that the exchange rate on the 'date of sale' should be considered. However, without proper clarification on that issue the date of sale can be the date of contract, purchase order, order confirmation or date of invoice, and depending on which is chosen, comparisons may differ and so does the dumping margin. Fifth, to obtain the margin of dumping, the weighted average normal value should be compared with a weighted average of export prices, or normal value should be compared with the export price on transaction-to-transaction basis. But under certain circumstances, the weighted average normal value can also be compared to the export price for a specific transaction, which might lead to higher dumping margins. In addition, in computing a weighted average dumping margin, the agreement is unclear about how negative dumping should be treated. Sixth, if preliminary investigations establish dumping and injury, exporters may submit voluntary price undertakings to revise prices or cease exports at dumped prices. In practice, price undertakings are anything but voluntary, often involving arm-twisting policies. Seventh, although the agreement says that ADD cannot exceed the margin of dumping, it is unclear about whether ADD should be equal to the margin of dumping or less than that (e.g. equal to the margin of injury). Eighth, since ADD are product and source specific, they can be circumvented by changing the customs tariff classification, or by slightly altering the description of the product (i.e., to place it in another tariff category) or by completing a part of the production process in the country of import or in any third country. The ADA has virtually nothing to say on such circumvention.

Finally, when dumping occurs, users of the dumped product (industrial users of the semi-processed items or the final consumers) benefit from lower prices. These represent welfare gains from dumping. The Uruguay Round ADA, for the first time, stipulates that such gainer parties (i.e., the users) should be consulted before imposing the ADD. But this evidence is only on dumping, injury and causality, not in terms of welfare gains that accrue to consumers resulting in welfare losses. Now given the present provisions of the ADA and clauses that allow subjectivity, it is the easiest thing in the world to prove dumping. But interpreted literally, since all other relevant factors must be excluded, it is virtually impossible to demonstrate injury or causality. In operational terms, most countries, therefore, establish dumping and have a perfunctory proof of injury or causality. India has faced a number of the problems described above, and is actively highlighting them in the negotiating forums over the last decade (see Annex A at the end).[5]

From 1 January 1995, GATT was subsumed under the WTO (World Trade Organization), following the Uruguay Round (1986-1994) of negotiations. Since January 1995, six WTO Ministerial Meetings have been held. The Fourth Ministerial in Doha (2001) was particularly important with launching of the Doha Development Agenda (DDA), although it did not contemplate any major changes to the ADA. Under the head of WTO Rules, it was stated, "In the light of experience and of the increasing application of these instruments by Members, we agree to negotiations aimed at clarifying and improving disciplines under the Agreements on Implementation of

---

5. See, *India and the WTO*, Vol. 1, No. 4 April 1999.

Article VI of the GATT 1994 ... while preserving the basic concepts, principles and effectiveness...and taking into account the needs of developing and least-developed participants. In the initial phase of the negotiations, participants will indicate the provisions, including disciplines on trade distorting practices, that they seek to clarify and improve in the subsequent phase." Had the Fifth Ministerial in Cancun in 2003 not failed, there would have been some mid-term stocktaking of these negotiations. At Doha, there was also a Ministerial Declaration on implementation-related issues and concerns which agreed that, "investigating authorities shall examine with special care any application for the initiation of an anti-dumping investigation where an investigation of the same product from the same member resulted in a negative finding within the 365 days prior to the filing of the application and that, unless this pre-initiation examination indicates that circumstances have changed, the investigation shall not proceed." It further vowed to recognise that, "while Article 15 of the Agreement on the Implementation of Article VI of the General Agreement on Tariffs and Trade 1994 is a mandatory provision, the modalities for its application would benefit from clarification. Accordingly, the Committee on Anti-Dumping Practices is instructed, through its working group on Implementation, to examine this issue and to draw up appropriate recommendations within 12 months on how to operationalise this provision." It also directed time-bound review of several provisions under ADA:

> ... Article 5.8 of the Agreement on the Implementation of Article VI of the General Agreement on Tariffs and Trade 1994 does not specify the time-frame to be used in determining the volume of dumped imports, and that this lack of specificity creates uncertainties in the implementation of the provision. The Committee on Anti-Dumping Practices is instructed, through its working group on Implementation, to study this issue and draw up recommendations within 12 months, with a view to ensuring the maximum possible predictability and objectivity in the application of time frames.
>
> ... Article 18.6 of the Agreement on the Implementation of Article VI of the General Agreement on Tariffs and Trade 1994 requires the Committee on Anti-Dumping Practices to review annually the implementation and operation of the Agreement taking into account the objectives thereof. The Committee on Anti-Dumping Practices is instructed to draw up guidelines for the improvement of annual reviews and to report its views and recommendations to the General Council for subsequent decision within 12 months.

However the initial deadline as prescribed by the DDA (January 2005) has already been missed. The Sixth Ministerial held in Hong

Kong in December 2005 has stressed the need for speedy agreement among members on the unfinished modalities in agricultural as well as industrial products. Nonetheless given the discontent among the members over other issues like agriculture, the ADA was not a priority area. Broadly speaking, the Hong Kong Ministerial declaration has set the stage for negotiations on the following concern areas:

> ... negotiations on anti-dumping should, as appropriate, clarify and improve the rules regarding, *inter alia*, (a) determinations of dumping, injury and causation, and the application of measures; (b) procedures governing the initiation, conduct and completion of anti-dumping investigations, including with a view to strengthening due process and enhancing transparency; and (c) the level, scope and duration of measures, including duty assessment, interim and new shipper reviews, sunset, and anti-circumvention proceedings;
>
> ... in the negotiations on anti-dumping, the Negotiating Group on Rules has been discussing in detail proposals on such issues as determinations of injury/causation, the lesser duty rule, public interest, transparency and due process, interim reviews, sunset, duty assessment, circumvention, the use of facts available, limited examination and all others rates, dispute settlement, the definition of dumped imports, affiliated parties, product under consideration, and the initiation and completion of investigations, and that this process of discussing proposals before the Group or yet to be submitted will continue after Hong Kong.

Looking at the stream of events, the current debate over ADA could broadly be summarised as follows. While industrial tariff reform in developed countries enhance the level of market access, increased usage of protectionist policies like anti-dumping investigations, especially through back-to-back investigations on the same product totally nullifies that. Policy substitution is understandable in a situation where tariffs are being disciplined, since protectionism will not go away. Therefore the developing countries are demanding several things to tackle that including extension of special and different treatment (SDT) to them, increase in the *de minimis* margin as well as the figure for 'negligible' imports from developing countries, strict observance of the lesser duty rule, increase in the required percentage of domestic industry applying for initiating investigations against developing country exports, etc. Also it is argued that if a dispute settlement panel arrives at a conclusion that is different from the conclusion arrived at by the country imposing ADD, the panel must be allowed to overturn the imposition of ADD.

As mentioned earlier, from an Indian perspective, similar to other developing countries, the ADA has two angles. First, Indian exporters are facing anti-dumping investigations on several key export items abroad. However, more than the imposition of ADD, the process of investigations constitutes a non-tariff barrier (NTB) and the associated procedural hassles significantly impedes market access for Indian exports. A point needs to be made here about the almost universal classification of ADD under the head of NTBs, thus, reinforcing the argument that there is policy substitution from protection through tariffs to protection through NTBs. Conceptually, it is not clear why ADD should be called NTBs. Any kind of duties are essentially price-based measures. Presumably, the argument is that anti-dumping investigations and resultant transaction costs act as NTBs, but this distinction between the two aspects of anti-dumping is rarely made. This angle of anti-dumping has always been important. On this, there are problems in demonstrating costs of production because of the non-transparent nature of the indirect tax system.[6] The complete VAT (value added tax), integrated for goods and services, is a long way off and such problems also occur in the context of the subsidies and countervailing measures agreement. Second, products coming from other countries may be dumped into India (e.g. the alleged dumping of a wide range of products from China). Historically, with high import duties and quantitative restrictions (QRs) on imports, this was not that important for India. But with reforms, import duties have been brought down and QRs have been phased-out, barring those retained on Article XX and XXI grounds. Therefore, dumping into India has also become important. In the recent years, India has become a major user of anti-dumping investigations, as well as some other NTBs through standards.[7]

The Current Volume

While the form that a new and modified Article VI should take can be debated, this is the background against which the eight chapters included in this volume need to be considered. While the EU and the

6. There are additional problems of Indian exporters not maintaining proper books of accounts or these not conforming to international accounting standards. If they are maintained, they are not carefully separated into domestic sales and export sales and there is the additional problem of joint production.
7. However, care must be taken in comparing data on India's use of anti-dumping investigations. These originate either through WTO, or through India's internal data generation system, although the latter feeds into the former. The classification systems are not the same. For instance, if there is an investigation involving multiple countries, the Indian reporting system classifies this as a single anti-dumping investigation. But in WTO's reporting system, this is counted multiple times, each country counting as a separate investigation.

US are the 'seasoned' users of anti-dumping provisions against imports, developing countries like India, Turkey and South Africa have already emerged as 'new' users, and these countries are currently initiating a significant number of anti-dumping investigations as compared to the corresponding figures a decade back. Given this new trend, the volume starts with the analysis on the developing countries, the first three chapters discussing the scenario in India, Turkey and South Africa respectively. The intensity of intra-developing country anti-dumping investigations is already a serious concern, and hence the fourth chapter of the volume focuses on this issue. The concern with the anti-dumping scenario in developed countries comes next and the fifth and the sixth chapters describe the policies and practices followed by the US and the EU respectively. The seventh chapter attempts to identify the economics behind China's emergence as a traditional 'victim', in the light of the huge number of anti-dumping investigations it faces, both in developed and developing countries. Finally, although the numbers of anti-dumping investigations are quite high, several chapters in the volume note that not all of them are challenged in the WTO Dispute Settlement Body (DSB) owing to various reasons. Looking into the DSB rulings, the last chapter attempts to identify the clauses within the ADA, which are most frequently violated.

The first chapter by K.D. Raju briefly highlights the problems associated with the ADA and then goes on to discuss the Indian case, noting that the government policies ultimately benefit only a handful of players at the cost of downstream industries and consumer welfare. The chapter further notes that instead of protecting import-competing industries, the focus should rather be on the welfare of small scale industries (SSIs), who are affected more by the imposition of ADD since they are forced to purchase raw materials from the local monopolies for a higher price than the same in the international market. Furthermore, the average period taken by India for carrying out the investigations and imposing final duties is substantially long as compared to other WTO members, thereby adding to the costs. The chapter concludes by calling for reform of the protectionist mindset against imports.

The second chapter by Cengiz Bahçekapili and Murat Çokgezen observes that the procedure of calculating normal value in order to determine the presence and the extent of dumping is getting increasingly protectionist and in that background it analyses the concern with respect to Turkish policies over 1996 to mid 2005. The chapter notes that the controversial nature of the acknowledged methods for factual determination of normal value under the GATT Agreement is a key concern area. On top of it, the GATT Agreement itself and the anti-dumping regulations of several members have a wide range of open-ended issues and legally ill-defined grey areas, creating rooms for official authorities to make unfair and biased decisions. Looking into the anti-dumping investigations initiated by Turkey, the chapter noted arbitrary and biased decisions made by the Turkish authorities, mostly in three broad categories—selecting 'appropriate' third country, determining a 'like product' and generalisation of product categories. Interestingly, the chapter noted that in several cases where the Turkish authorities detected dumping and imposed duties, using an alternative methodology would have established negative dumping margins. This led the authors to recommend introducing reforms in the methods of calculating normal value and bringing clarity of the complex definitions, or alternatively, dismantling of the anti-dumping regulations altogether.

The third chapter by Nicola Theron notes the increase in anti-dumping investigations since the conclusion of the Uruguay Round, and attributes this to switching to newer forms of trade-restrictive instruments in the absence of the traditional policies. The chapter looks at various concern areas within the ADA as followed by select member countries, e.g. the investigating procedures, definition of interested parties, the practice of settling constructed normal values, determining material injury, injury margins and the lesser duty rule, causation and finally confidentiality, with special reference to South Africa, who has adopted a simplified version of the GATT ADA, in each case. The author notes that although the anti-dumping initiations by South Africa have increased in recent years, the procedure followed by the country is generally not very highly trade distorting. The chapter concludes that in future it will be necessary to discipline the growing trend in anti-dumping investigation, possibly through introduction of a more comprehensive anti-circumvention measures prescribed by the WTO.

The presence of high barriers on developing country exports in developed country markets is a well-known fact, which stresses the need to boost intra-developing country trade in no uncertain terms. Therefore the growing intra-developing country anti-dumping investigations might pose a serious threat to the multilateral trading system. In this background, the fourth chapter by Kofi Oteng Kufuor attempts to analyse the reason behind the emergence of more and more developing countries as leading users of this provision and explore the possible corrective measures. The chapter terms the current scenario to be a marriage of convenience; while the domestic import-competing industries in developing countries are demanding protection on the face of increasing WTO-induced import liberalisation, the elaborate procedure involving anti-dumping actions provide a perfect opportunity of institutional self-preservation to the public servants there. Hence the rise in intra-developing country anti-dumping investigations, and the fact that the developing countries hardly approach the GATT/WTO panels owing to various reasons further compounds the problem. The major recommendations of the chapter include creation of new, accountable, and transparent trade policy-making institutions by the developing countries that reflect the national interest rather than parochial interests, enactment of anti-dumping legislation by all WTO members to promote certainty in anti-dumping investigations, etc. among other means. It further argues in favour of a greater role for developing country regional organisations, while stressing the need for building up the capacity of civil society and consumer organisations in this regard.

In the fifth chapter, Brink Lindsey and Daniel Ikenson concentrate on the rhetoric and the reality of US anti-dumping law. Analysing the methodologies applied for dumping determination, the study concludes that the level playing field or fair competition argument is nothing but a decoy, and anti-dumping law too often ends up penalising normal commercial practices having nothing to do with anyone's definition of unfair trade. While the procedure is supposed to be used as a remedy for market distortions caused by policies followed by entities located abroad, in practice, it fails, repeatedly and at multiple levels, to distinguish between normal commercial pricing practices and those that actually reflect market-distorting policies. This is supported by the argument that even when such pricing evidence is found, that usually has little to do with market distortions. Not only does US practice of anti-dumping law have little to do with the rhetoric of ensuring a level playing field, in practice it simply encourages lobbying for protection. The point is that this is sanctioned by the ADA. The chapter argues that if true awareness about the impact of imposing anti-dumping investigations among the consumers increases, it will be much difficult for the proponents of this provision (mainly import-competing industries) to be openly supportive towards it.

The sixth chapter by Fredrik Erixon mentions that few countries today, and the EU in particular, bothers to investigate in detail the actual impact of dumping and the consequence for consumers. Although, the setting is somewhat different, the finding of the chapter closely resemble the same of the earlier chapter on the US. The EU practice has moved away from the original purpose of anti-dumping law and has become nothing but a common protectionist measure. The study notes that the methodology followed by the EU for determination of dumping does not properly consider whether the lower price in question is actually dumping or normal business strategy. In addition, the fact that the Council of Ministers, i.e., to say, a forum of elected politicians decides upon definite anti-dumping actions; leaves enough rooms for political considerations rather than economic ones to capture the entire procedure. Furthermore, the recent changes in voting pattern for the final determination, where abstentions of the members count as a vote in favour of imposing an anti-dumping measure rather than against it, made the imposition of the final duty on imported products all the more certain. The impact of the EU anti-dumping initiations on developing country exports is a major concern; it is observed that during 2003 and 2004, 100 and 86 per cent of the new initiations were against the former group respectively. The chapter notes, although the EU is in favour of reforming the anti-dumping practices in principle, it is unlikely that the unfair use of this provision is going to be curbed in a major way in coming future.

The seventh chapter by Yuefen Li examines how the inherent weakness and loopholes of anti-dumping laws have allowed multinational enterprises to use it as a weapon to squeeze out new market entrants and strengthen monopoly; with a less outright condemnation of the Anti-Dumping Agreement. Though the benefits of China's trade expansion have been distributed much more broadly than some early industrialisers, it has emerged as the number one target of anti-dumping investigations in the world. Being a new and relatively efficient producer, rivalry in the world market may be one important reason behind it. In part, the answer lies in China's export success, despite China not having attracted enough FDI and multinational enterprises (MNEs) so as to jump the ADA, so to speak. On the other hand, China's development stage and its trade structure also place it at a disadvantage when it comes to anti-dumping activities. The problems are likely to be aggravated further by the extensive safeguard provisions included in China's WTO accession commitments, which requires China to be treated, for anti-dumping purposes, as a non-market economy till 2016. And finally, there is inadequate Chinese legal capacity to defend itself against anti-dumping investigations initiated by trade partners. The chapter suggests that in the long run, it is necessary for China to shift its export basket away from anti-dumping-intensive sectors by upgrading from standard products to highly differentiated ones.

The eighth and final chapter by Debashis Chakraborty refers to of the protectionist arguments, and then focusing on the anti-dumping cases lodged at DSB, attempts to identify the articles and sub-articles of the agreement, the violation of which due to ambiguity are creating major problems for the exporting countries. It is observed that while the alleged violations are spread over the entire ADA, the proven frequent violations notably include determination of dumping and their impacts on the domestic industry, thereby supporting gross misuse of the basic provisions. Furthermore, looking into the anti-dumping cases involving India, and the changing perspective of the country in this issue, the future concern areas are noted. Finally on the basis of the observations, the chapter briefly comments on the future negotiating agenda on reforms of the ADA.

What is the justification of this volume? As the previous discussion points out, the DDA contemplates nothing beyond clarifying and improving of the existing disciplines. The analysis of all eight chapters in the volume adds credence to the contention that this is hardly going to meet the current level of requirement of having a systemic change in the ADA. There is consensus across all eight chapters that more substantial changes are needed in the ADA, although there is a lack of precision about what should be done if Article VI is ultimately dumped. Given the current political economy within the WTO, this first-best solution is unlikely to materialise sooner or later. But as a second-best option, the chapters of the current volume strongly endorse the argument that one needs much more than mere clarification and improvement of the ADA. Indeed that is topic for another volume!

1

India's Involvement in Anti-Dumping Cases in the First Decade of WTO

K.D. RAJU

Introduction

Given the fast growing trade and liberalisation in most of the economies of the world, anti-dumping duty laws and policy have reached a position of vital importance and is a recurring subject of debate in the international trade negotiations. The debate between 'free traders' and 'protectionists' may be analysed carefully. The rules on dumping procedure had been incorporated in the WTO Agreement on Anti-dumping (ADA) for protecting domestic industry against unfair trade practices. However, nowadays many WTO members use this law as a popular substitute for traditional barriers and a political shield to protect domestic interests. Although designed as a corrective mechanism against unfair trade, it has currently been hijacked for protectionist purposes.

Trade remedies are laws used by countries to mitigate the impacts of various trade-distorting practices on domestic industry. Dumping is condemned in WTO as an unfair trade practice. Therefore, anti-dumping laws provide relief to domestic industries from foreign competition when there is a consequent injury to the domestic industry by such imports. The GATT and WTO have been fairly successful in reducing tariff levels, but the regulatory protection is still continuing in the form of anti-dumping duties. Lowering tariffs and reducing protectionism is like draining a swamp; the WTO mandated draining of all protectionisms. However, the stumps in the water are still growing even in the era of 'globalisation'. The members have to gear up to fight against the frictional use of anti-dumping protectionism.

Dumping and anti-dumping issues are getting a lot of attention recently, mainly motivated by two developments. First, while the number of anti-dumping petitions has increased in the recent past, only a small percentage of the investigations are ending in actual imposition of duties. This is mainly due to mere filing of a petition that benefits the domestic industry by harassing the foreign exporter, which may lead to price undertakings and settlements. Second, incorporating industrial organisation aspects into trade theory has given a new impetus to the analysis of the dumping phenomenon.[1]

Although dumping cases are quite a sensitive topic in the international trading system nowadays, very few countries were the users of this measure up to 1980s. During 1990s the number of countries using this measure to block imports has increased. The establishment of WTO in 1995 and adoption of the WTO agreements including Article VI (popularly known as ADA) of the General Agreement on Tariffs and Trade (GATT), changed the whole scenario. Now the entire regime is controlled by this international agreement. Since the adoption of WTO ADA, the number of initiations shot up amazingly all over the world. The protectionism is no longer the monopoly of developed countries now. The trend has affected developing countries as well. India has emerged as a prominent user of this protectionist measure along with other WTO members. It is also interesting to note that most of her initiations are against other developing countries; and the exports of a non-market economy like China are among the most affected ones.

Internationally 'dumping' is defined differently. In a layman's view, it is sales of goods in the market for a lower price. In anti-dumping law, a product is considered to be dumped if its export price is lower than its normal value. The export price and normal value is defined according to the national law of various WTO members after taking into account special situations of the concerned country. A fair comparison between normal value and export price has to be made for finding out the dumping margin. If the dumping margin is more than two per cent, anti-dumping duties can be imposed, otherwise it is considered as *de minimis*. Furthermore, dumping is not the sole criteria for imposing anti-dumping duties. Injury to the domestic industry and a causal relationship with dumping and injury must be established.

In India, anti-dumping cases are of recent origin, although the country included anti-dumping provisions in its statutes in 1985.

1. Thusnelda, Tivig and Uwe Walz (2000). "Market Share, Cost Based Dumping and Anti-dumping Policy", *The Canadian Journal of Economics*, Vol. 33, No. 1, pp. 69-86.

Perhaps this is owing to the prevalence of high tariffs on imports in India until 1991, since when gradual tariff reform took place. Quantitative restrictions also played a crucial role in preventing increasing influx of goods into the Indian market during eighties, thereby limiting the use of anti-dumping provisions. Notably, India initiated its first anti-dumping investigation in 1992. India further amended its provisions in accordance with the ADA in 1995. Sections 9A, 9AA, 9B and 9C were included in the Customs Tariff Act 1975.

Recent Developments

Since the establishment of the WTO in 1995 to December 2004, out of the 149 Members, 98 Members have initiated 2840 investigations. During this period, India initiated 426 initiations and thus became the leader in this field. The US is in the second position (366) followed by EU (327), Argentina (204), South Africa (197), Australia (179), Canada (134), China (123), Turkey (109), and Mexico (85) respectively. This set constitutes the top 10 initiators. China is the victim country with 469 initiations against it from 1995 to December 2005. Korea is in the second position (218) followed by the US (162), Chinese Taipei (160), Japan (125), India (124), Indonesia (121), Thailand (111), Russia (97) and Brazil (89) respectively.

In 2005, 29 Members reported initiating a total of 191 new investigations, compared with 213 initiations in the corresponding period of 2004. A total of 28 Members applied 131 new final anti-dumping measures in 2005, compared to 151 new measures applied in 2004. During the second half of 2005, 27 of the 82 new initiations were opened by developed Members, and 27 of the 76 new final measures were applied by developed Members. This compares with 42 new initiations opened and 24 new measures applied by developed members during the first half of 2004. In the second half of 2005, for the first time in the history of WTO, China surpassed India and initiated 13 investigations. On the other hand, China remains the most frequent subject of the new investigations, with 33 initiations directed at its exports during July-December 2005. This is up from 24 initiations during the corresponding period of 2004. China is followed by Malaysia, Indonesia, Korea, Chinese Taipei, Thailand, US, European Communities, India, Japan, Hong Kong, China and Vietnam. This set constitutes the top 10 countries as victims of dumping.

The products that were the most frequent subject of the new investigations during July-December 2005 were in the chemicals sector (17 initiations), followed by base metals (15 initiations) and plastics (12 initiations). China is the victim with 13 of the total 17 initiations in the chemical sector. Plastic sector and base metals are also targeted. The percentages of final measures (imposing duties) are also increasing among the WTO members.

The countries mentioned above constitute the top 10 anti-dumping initiators in the WTO, jointly contributing roughly 77 per cent of the total initiations. The group of three, India, US and the EU alone contributed around 40 per cent of the total investigations. It is observed that the traditional users[2] contributed only 36 per cent of the cases, while the rest of the Members have initiated the remaining 64 per cent. It is interesting to note that until 1980 these traditional users initiated 95 per cent of the total initiations in the GATT system, while the high income countries contributed 41 per cent of the initiations.[3] This implies that developing countries are emerging as the majority users of this provision in the WTO at present. Figure 1.1 shows the annual trend in initiations of anti-dumping investigations during 1980-2005.

Substantial Dumping Issues at WTO

Recently WTO members are getting increasingly concerned about the spurt in anti-dumping actions.[4] On several occasions the aggrieved Members have approached the WTO dispute settlement body (DSB) for redressal of their grievance. Presently, majority of the cases brought before the DSB is on anti-dumping issue. Many Members have complained on the misuse of this provision for partisan and protectionist purposes. Some decisions of the DSB substantiate this position. In *EU-India Bed Linen* case,[5] the Appellate Body (AB) held that the "zeroing" methodology used by EU for calculation of dumping margin is incompatible with the ADA provisions. The EU and US popularly uses this zeroing methodology, which eliminates

2. This included the EU, US, Australia and Canada.
3. According to the World Bank classification these countries include Australia, Canada, Israel, Japan, Rep. of Korea, New Zealand, European Union and the United States.
4. Figure 1.1 gives the fluctuations of anti-dumping investigations from 1980–2005.
5. European Communities—Anti-dumping Duties on Imports of Cotton-Type Bed Linen from India, WT/DS141/AB/R, March 1, 2001.

Figure 1.1

Anti-Dumping Initiations from 1980 to 2004 All Over the World

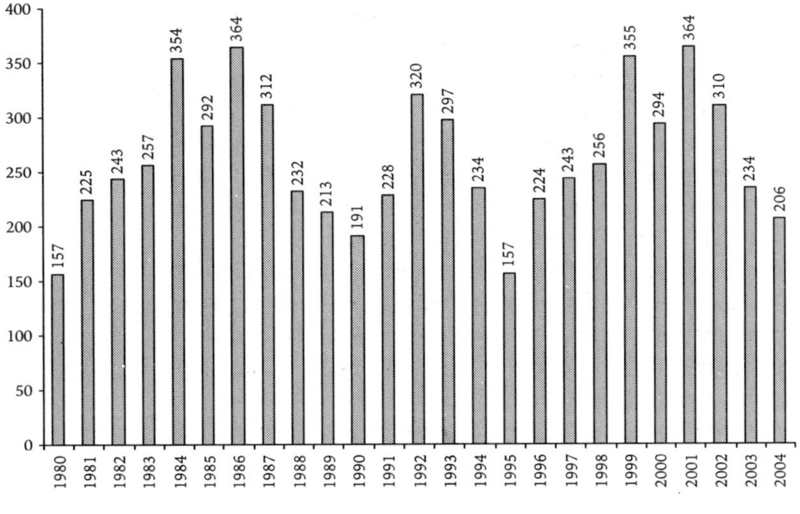

Source: GATT and WTO Secretariat.

negative dumping margin from the calculation of 'dumping margin'. As a consequence, the investigation always leads to positive dumping margin in calculations. If there are only positive dumping margins, it does not make any impact on calculations, but zeroing of negative dumping margins as practiced by these countries is a problematic issue. In *Softwood Lumber* dispute brought by Canada, the WTO Panel held that:

> ... the US has violated Article 2.4.2 of the ADA by not taking into account all comparable export transactions when DOC calculated the overall margin of dumping as Article 2.4.2 requires that the existence of margins of dumping has to be established for softwood lumber on the basis of a comparison of the weighted-average-normal value with the weighted average of prices of all comparable export transactions, that is, for all transactions involving all types of products under investigation.[6]

India is a strong supporter of abolition of the 'zeroing' methodology. However, it has also been a user of this methodology in

6. United States-Final Dumping Determination on Softwood Lumber from Canada, WT/DS264, April 13 2004, p. 128.

some of the cases dealt by the Directorate General of Anti Dumping (DGAD) under domestic compulsions.[7] It is interesting to note that the EU, proponent of 'zeroing' methodology approached the DSB against the use of zeroing by the US in 31 different anti-dumping cases.[8] The DSB may rule against US, as a clear precedent has been set by the decision in *EU-India Bed Linen* case. However, even after an adverse decision against 'zeroing' there is every possibility that the US might argue in favour of zeroing in individual cases. This is mainly due to the ambiguity in Article 2.4.2 of the ADA. The AB ruled in *Bed Linen* case that zeroing prevents average-to-average comparisons, while the ADA permits individual-to-average comparisons in certain circumstances. Therefore if dumping is calculated otherwise like average-to-individual comparisons, there is every possibility of finding dumping. These will be completely ADA-consistent. It means, even after the adverse ruling against zeroing, the ambiguity still remains, creating room for future disputes. Table 1.1 shows how the 'zeroing' methodology works in a representative investigation, ultimately leading to detection of dumping.

Table 1.1

Zeroing Methodology

Product Code	*Net EM Price*	*Net HM Price*	*Unit Margin*	*Quantity*	*Total Value*
1	$1.00	$0.50	-$0.50	100	$100
2	$1.00	$1.00	$0.00	100	$100
3	$1.00	$1.00	$0.00	100	$100
4	$1.00	$1.00	$0.00	100	$100
5	$1.00	$1.50	$0.50	100	$100
Total Margin Without Zeroing			$0		
Total Margin Using Zeroing		$50			
Total Value					$500
Final Dumping Margin					10.00%

Source : Author's own calculation based on a hypothetical case.

Note : EM-Export Market;
HM-Home Market.

7. One of the former Indian Ambassador to the WTO, in his personal conversation with this author admitted that India has used this methodology in anti-dumping cases.
8. Ikenson, Daniel (2004). "Zeroing In: Anti-dumping's Flawed Methodology under Fire", CATO Institute, *Trade Policy Bulletin* No. 11, April 27.

Back-to-back investigations are another menace faced by the developing countries. The complainant in EU-India Bed Linen dispute, the EUROCOTTON was unable to manage the required support for its first application in 1994 and the investigation was terminated in 1996. The second investigation was started immediately after 20 days of the termination of first investigation, showing the misuse of the provisions. An investigation is more effective than actual anti-dumping duties in many cases. This is mainly due to the 'chilling effect' and harassment of the importers in the course of the investigation. Therefore, there is an urgent need to induct a new provision in the ADA, which would prohibit initiation of a fresh investigation for one year after the establishment of non-dumping in a previous investigation.[9]

Article 15 of the ADA provides for special and differential treatment (SDT) for the developing countries.[10] India claimed this privilege in *EU-India Bed Linen* dispute. However, EU stated that they considered India's request, but found no other constructive remedies. It is pointed out that Article 15 is a 'soft law' provision within the 'hard law' obligations under WTO agreements. The Doha Ministerial Declaration also agreed with the sentiments of developing country members and decided to review this provision.[11]

Article 6.8 and Annex II of the ADA authorises the use of "facts available," when a party refuses access to or does not provide necessary information within a reasonable period of time or when a party significantly impedes the process of investigation. In many cases this provision is misused by the investigation authorities. In the United States-Anti-Dumping Measures on *Certain Hot-rolled Steel Products from Japan* dispute;[12] the Panel held that the US investigating authorities violated the concerned provisions of ADA. It is not clear as to under what circumstances the 'facts available' provision can be

9. Raju, K.D. (2004-2). "The WTO Appellate Body Reports on Anti-dumping: A Critical Review", *Indian Journal of International Law*, Vol. 44, pp. 260-291.

10. Article 15 states, "It is recognized that special regard must be given by developed country Members to the special situation of the developing country Members when considering the application of anti-dumping measures under this Agreement. Possibilities of constructive remedies provided for by this Agreement shall be explored before applying anti-dumping duties where they would affect the essential interests of developing country Members."

11. WTO Doha Ministerial Declaration adopted on November 14, 2001, para. 44, WT/MIN (01)/DEC/1.

12. WT/DS184/R.

used. In *India-Steel Plate*[13] dispute also, the US authorities rejected the submitted data and took recourse to this provision for a decision in favour of US steel industry. In this case also the Panel rejected the argument of the US authorities. All these concerns call for an urgent need to standardise and simplify the procedures for submitting required trade data.

Dumping Cases in India

The amendment and inclusion of Sections 9A, 9AA, 9B and 9C to the Customs Tariff Act (1975) was made in 1995 in accordance with the obligations under the ADA. In 1992, India initiated its first dumping investigation on PVC Resin exported from Brazil, Mexico, Korea and US. Gradually the number of cases increased even to 81 in 2002 and afterwards gradually decreased to 21 in 2004.[14] It is interesting to note that out of 400 initiations,[15] only 167 initiations ended up in investigations and in 142 cases final decisions have been made.[16] Preliminary findings are over in 6 cases and 10 cases are pending for final/interim decisions. Only 9 cases have been closed after investigations. It means that only 42 per cent of the applications have ended in investigations and only 5 per cent applications stand closed without imposing any duties.[17]

Between 1992 and 2004, appeals have been filed in 63 cases by various interested parties in the CESTAT (Customs, Excise & Servicce Tax Appellate) out of which, final rulings has been made by CESTAT in 46 cases. Thirty-one cases have been decided in favour of the Designated Authority (DA), orders of the DA have been modified in 11 cases and in 4 cases the orders have been quashed. During this period, 32 writ petitions have been filed in various High Courts. In 2 cases, matters have been transferred to Supreme Court and 14 cases are pending for orders. The number of appeals filed in the Supreme Court since 1992-2004 is 18. The Supreme Court passed orders in 5 cases and 13 cases are pending for orders at the Supreme Court level.

---

13. *United States-Anti-Dumping and Countervailing Measures on Steel Plate from India,* WT/DS/206/R, June 28, 2002.
14. The WTO figure is 18 in 2004, but in the DGAD Annual Report, the figure is only 14 initiations.
15. See Figure 1.2.
16. See DGAD Annual Report 2003-04, Chapter 3.
17. Ninety-five per cent of the investigations are ended in imposing duties. It is a high rate as compared to the other WTO members.

Figure 1.2

Anti-Dumping Initiations by India and US—A Comparative Analysis (1995-2005)

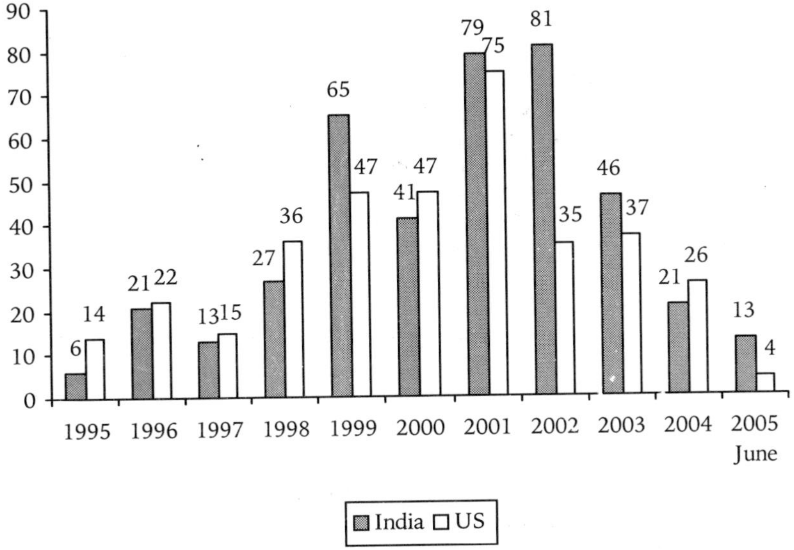

Source: WTO Secretariat (2005).

In India, disposal of cases in the CESTAT is speedier than other countries. For circumventing a speedy remedy, many petitions are filed before the High Courts (under Article 226 of the Indian Constitution) and Supreme Court of India. The number of cases pending before the High Courts and Supreme Court shows that the judicial system in India is slower than any other administrative functionaries. This is causing disruptions in trade for the interim period and there is an urgent need to have a special bench of the Supreme Court for this purpose. However, it is observed from Figure 1.2 that the number of initiations in India is declining over the last three years, although the decline is relatively less steep as compared to the trend in the US.

Table 1.2

Indian and US Anti-Dumping Initiations by Product Types—A Comparative Analysis

WTO Product Category No.	*Products*	*Indian Initiations*	*US Initiations*
I	Live animals; animal products.	0	15
II	Vegetable products.	0	12
III	Animal or vegetable fats and oils and their cleavage products; prepared edible fats; animal or vegetable waxes.	1	0
IV	Prepared foodstuffs; beverages, spirits and vinegar; tobacco and manufactured tobacco substitutes.	0	6
V	Mineral products.	10	8
VI	Products of the chemical or allied industries.	178	45
VII	Plastics and articles thereof; rubber and articles thereof.	60	29
VIII	Raw hides and skins, leather, furskins and articles thereof; saddlery and harness; travel goods, handbags and similar containers; articles of animal gut (other than silk-worm gut).	0	0
IX	Wood and articles of wood; wood charcoal; cork and articles of cork; manufactures of straw, of esparto or of other plaiting materials; basketware and wickerwork.	0	2
X	Pulp of wood or of other fibrous cellulosic material; recovered (waste and scrap) paper or paperboard; paper and paperboard and articles thereof.	14	3
XI	Textiles and textile articles.	48	8
XII	Footwear, headgear, umbrellas, sun umbrellas, walking-sticks, seat-sticks, whips, riding-crops and parts thereof; prepared feathers and articles made therewith; artificial flowers; articles of human hair.	1	0
XIII	Articles of stone, plaster, cement, asbestos, mica or similar materials; ceramic products; glass and glassware.	9	2
XIV	Natural or cultured pearls, precious or semi-precious stones, precious metals, metals clad with precious metal and articles thereof; imitation jewellery; coin thereof; imitation jewellery; coin.	0	0

Contd. ...

...Contd. ...

WTO Product Category No.	*Products*	*Indian Initiations*	*US Initiations*
XV	Base metals and articles of base metal.	49	205
XVI	Machinery and mechanical appliances; electrical equipment; parts thereof; sound recorders and reproducers, television image and sound recorders and reproducers, and parts and accessories of such articles.	33	17
XVII	Vehicles, aircraft, vessels and associated transport equipment.	0	4
XVIII	Optical, photographic, cinematographic, measuring, checking, precision, medical or surgical instruments and apparatus; clocks and watches; musical instruments; parts and accessories thereof.	3	0
XIX	Arms and ammunition; parts and accessories thereof.		
XX	Miscellaneous manufactured articles.	2	2
XXI	Works of art, collectors' pieces and antiques.		
...	Unknown.	4	0
	Total	**412**	**358**

Source: WTO Secretariat, 2005.

Table 1.2 shows a comparison between Indian and US initiations of anti-dumping investigations by product categories. It is observed from the table that India initiated 43 per cent of the total cases in petrochemicals, chemicals and other products. Second most affected category is plastics and rubber products (16 per cent). Textiles and textile products and base metals constitute 15 per cent and 11.5 per cent of the total investigations respectively. Given the presence of various corporate entities in the Indian petrochemical industry, it seems that the investigations are actually helping these players at the cost of downstream industries and compromising on consumer welfare. Injury and definition to the domestic industry needs to be re-defined in favour of consumer interests rather than corporate interests. India is taking an average period of 390 days for undertaking its investigations and imposing final duties. It is a long period when compared to other Members.

It is observed from Table 1.3 that China is the major victim of Indian anti-dumping initiations (nearly 20 per cent of the total initiations). Nine per cent of the cases are initiated against the EU followed by Taiwan (7%), Korea (7%), US (5%) and Japan (5%). Among other major affected trade partners, Singapore, Thailand, Indonesia and Russia deserve special mention. It is surprising to note that while India has initiated 16 anti-dumping cases against Thailand, it on the other hand is actively negotiating for a free trade area between the two countries. Recently, EU has taken up nearly 25 cases to the DSB against India. China is also actively thinking to take India to the WTO over the anti-dumping initiations. So far, Russia is not a WTO member and it may not be able to take up the matter to the DSB. Now fighting anti-dumping cases always involve a huge cost and India, as a developing country, may not be able to afford defending all these cases in WTO. Instead of paying huge amount for hiring foreign lawyers, India should develop its own trained manpower in the country to defend its interests in WTO.[18]

Table 1.3

Top 10 Victims of Indian Initiations (January 1995- June 2005)

Sl. No	*Country*	*Number of Initiations*
1.	China P.R.	81
2.	EU	36
3.	Chinese Taipei	30
4.	Korea Rep.	29
5.	US	22
6.	Japan	20
7.	Singapore	18
8.	Russia	18
9.	Thailand	16
10.	Indonesia	16

Source: WTO Secretariat (2005).

Anti-dumping Initiations Against India

India is also facing a number of initiations from other WTO members. Since 1995-December 2004, India has faced 105 initiations. EU has initiated the maximum number of cases (27), followed by the

18. Raju, K.D. (2005). "Anti-dumping Protectionism 2005 and Beyond", in J.K. Mittal and K.D. Raju, (eds.), *The World Trade Organization and India: A Critical Study of Its First Decade*, New Delhi, New Era Law Publications.

South Africa (20), US (18), Indonesia (10), Turkey (7), Canada, and Argentina (5), Egypt and Australia (4 cases each), Korea and Brazil (3 cases each), Thailand, Trinidad and Tobago, China (2 cases each), while Malaysia, Peru and Poland contributed 1 case each. The scenario is shown with the help of Figure 1.3.

India has initiated 76 investigations against China, but China has initiated only 2 cases against India. During the same period, China faced 411 initiations by other Members, while it initiated only 99 investigations against others. It shows that there is no evidence of retaliation against those countries who are initiating cases against China. It is observed that four countries, namely the EU, the US, South Africa and Indonesia alone have initiated about 69 per cent of the total cases against India.

Figure 1.3

Anti-Dumping Initiations Against India—1995-2005 (Country-Wise)

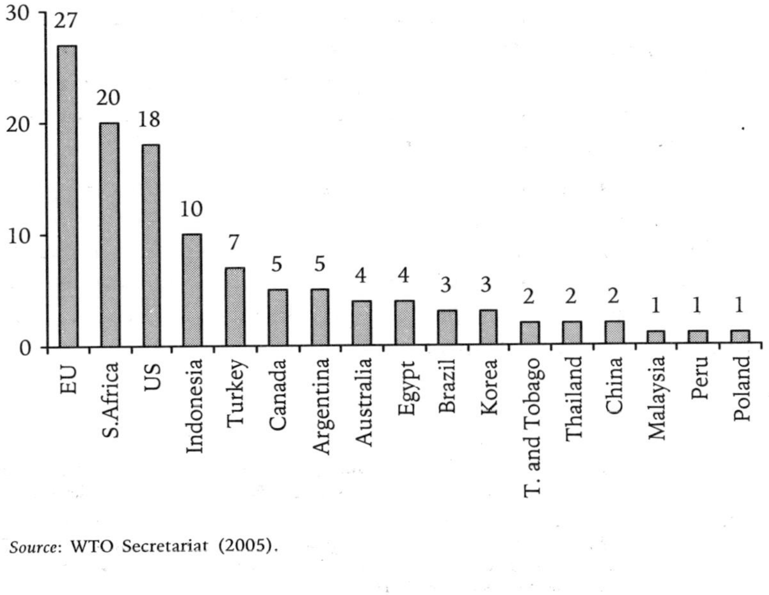

Source: WTO Secretariat (2005).

Conclusion

The anti-dumping regime at the WTO and domestic levels are presently at the crossroads. It has emerged as one of the most important trade remedy instrument at the international level.[19] The Members have never thought that anti-dumping disputes would rise to the present level when they concluded the Agreement in 1995. Since 1995, 321 cases have been initiated under the DSU, out of which more than 57 cases are in the anti-dumping stream alone. It seems the continuous drift towards liberalisation and import tariff-cuts in the Member countries compelled them to explore other avenues of protectionism. The petrochemical and steel industries have used anti-dumping measures frequently.

The rationale for using anti-dumping seems to be misplaced in the first decade of working of the international trading system.[20] The present investigative procedures are proved to be built in favour of domestic protectionist bias and used as a non-tariff barrier (NTB). The ADA provided numerous loopholes and latitudes for substantial manipulation at procedural levels. It is interesting to note that the common perception inherited from the Tokyo Round, until the establishment of the WTO, that the ADA is a 'rich man's remedy' is rapidly changing since many developing countries have become active users of anti-dumping investigations not only against developed countries but also against other developing countries.[21]

Various methodologies such as 'zeroing' and 'arms' length' in calculating dumping margin are fishy in nature and help the developed world for finding dumping always. The recent trend that the developing countries like India, South Africa and Indonesia are becoming pioneers in this field and most of the initiations are against developing countries is also alarming.

---

19. Now the protectionist battles are fought on an industry-by-industry basis at the domestic level and country-to-country basis before the WTO dispute settlement body.

20. Indiscriminate recourse to anti-dumping actions has caused alarm among researchers, analysts and administrators about its efficacy and misuse as a protection measure. The current anti-dumping practice created a paradoxical situation in which it is out of line with the spirit and philosophy of WTO.

21. UNCTAD, *Negotiating Anti-dumping and Settling Priorities Among Outstanding Implementation Issues in the Post-Doha Scenario: A First Examination in the Light of Recent Practice and DSU Jurisprudence*, UNCTAD/ITCD/TSB/Misc. 72, 2002.

Finger criticises the anti-dumping law as, "... the fox put in charge of the hen house: trade restrictions certified by GATT. The fox is clever enough not only to eat the hens, but also to convince the farmer that is the way things ought to be."[22] Anti-dumping supporters say it is for the benefit of the domestic industry. However, economists are finding it difficult to justify or claim any economic benefit or rationale behind imposing anti-dumping duties. Consumer organisations criticise that it takes away the consumer benefits such as choice of products and cost benefits.

It is observed that at the WTO level, countries talk about "level playing field," while at the domestic level justifying protectionism. This often has led to accusation about the use of anti-dumping actions in a protectionist manner with administrative authorities making arbitrary and politically motivated decisions.

To add to the problems, the anti-dumping agreement by design is somewhat ambiguous. Many countries want to reform the ADA to introduce more specificity and guidelines in the application of the trade remedy law. The DDA made it clear that the future agenda is to "clarify and improve" the ADA than to eliminate it.

In India, the trend is very clear and petrochemicals imports are always under threat from imposition of anti-dumping duties. The government should protect and concentrate more on the welfare of small scale industries (SSIs) and consumers rather than protecting the interests of big players in India. Due to the protectionism, downstream purchasers are forced to rely on local monopolies for raw materials at a higher price than the prevailing one in the international market.

In future, chances are high that China will surpass India in anti-dumping initiations as a retaliatory measure; at the same time Chinese textile goods is likely to meet more dumping investigations in the US and EU. The WTO cases will act as a deterrent against India for initiating more cases in future. There is a need to reform the prevailing lengthy and cumbersome administrative and judicial procedure in India. It is unlikely that the number of anti-dumping initiations all over the world would be reduced in the coming days substantially. This is mainly due to political reasons both in developed as well as developing countries.

---

22. Finger, Michael J. (1991). "The Origin and Evolution of Anti-Dumping Regulation", *World Bank Working Papers*, WPS 783, 23 October.

Annexure A-1.1

Anti-Dumping Initiations by Reporting Member
(01-01-95 to 30-06-2005)

Reporting Member	*1995*	*1996*	*1997*	*1998*	*1999*	*2000*	*2001*	*2002*	*2003*	*2004*	*2005 June*	*Total*
Argentina	27	22	14	8	23	45	26	14	1	12	1	**193**
Australia	5	17	42	13	24	15	23	16	8	9	2	**174**
Brazil	5	18	11	18	16	11	17	8	4	8	3	**119**
Bulgaria	0	0	0	0	0	0	0	1	0	0	0	**1**
Canada	11	5	14	8	18	21	25	5	15	11	0	**133**
Chile	4	3	0	2	0	5	0	0	0	0	0	**14**
China, P.R.	0	0	0	0	0	6	14	30	22	27	11	**110**
Chinese Taipei	0	0	0	0	0	3	3	0	2	0	0	**8**
Colombia	4	1	1	6	2	3	6	0	0	0	1	**26**
Costa Rica	0	4	1	1	0	0	0	0	0	0	0	**6**
Czech Republic	0	0	0	2	1	0	0	0	0	0	0	**3**
Ecuador	0	0	0	1	0	0	0	0	0	0	0	**1**
Egypt	0	0	7	14	5	1	7	3	1	0	7	**45**
European Community	33	25	41	22	65	32	28	20	7	30	15	**318**
Guatemala	0	1	0	0	0	0	0	0	0	0	0	**1**
India	**6**	**21**	**13**	**27**	**65**	**41**	**79**	**81**	**46**	**21**	13	**412**
Indonesia	0	11	5	8	8	3	4	4	13	4	0	**60**
Israel	5	6	3	7	0	1	4	0	0	1	3	**30**
Jamaica	0	0	0	0	0	1	1	1	1	0	0	**4**
Japan	0	0	0	0	0	0	2	0	0	0	0	**2**
Rep. of Korea	4	13	15	3	6	2	4	9	18	3	0	**76**
Latvia	0	0	0	0	0	0	1	6	0	0	0	**7**
Lithuania	0	0	0	0	1	6	0	0	0	0	0	**7**
Malaysia	3	2	8	1	2	0	1	5	6	3	4	**35**
Mexico	4	4	6	12	11	7	5	10	14	6	4	**82**
New Zealand	10	4	5	1	4	10	1	2	5	5	0	**46**
Nicaragua	0	0	0	2	0	0	0	0	0	0	0	**2**
Pakistan	0	0	0	0	0	0	0	0	3	3	0	**7**
Panama	0	0	0	2	0	0	0	0	0	0	0	2
Paraguay	0	0	0	0	1	0	0	0	0	0	0	**1**
Peru	2	7	2	3	8	1	8	12	5	7	3	**59**

Contd..

...Contd..

Reporting Member	*1995*	*1996*	*1997*	*1998*	*1999*	*2000*	*2001*	*2002*	*2003*	*2004*	*2005 June*	*Total*
Philippines	1	1	2	3	6	2	0	1	1	0	0	**17**
Poland	0	0	1	0	7	0	0	3	1	0	0	**12**
Slovenia	0	0	0	0	1	0	0	0	0	0	0	**1**
South Africa	16	33	23	41	16	21	6	4	8	5	17	**191**
Thailand	0	1	3	0	0	0	3	21	3	3	0	**34**
Trinidad and Tobago	0	1	0	4	3	1	1	0	2	0	0	**12**
Turkey	0	0	4	1	8	7	15	18	11	25	8	**97**
United States	14	22	15	36	47	47	75	35	37	26	4	**358**
Uruguay	0	0	1	0	0	1	4	0	0	0	0	**6**
Venezuela	3	2	6	10	7	1	1	1	0	0	0	**31**
Total for 01/01/95 - 31/12/04	**157**	**224**	**243**	**256**	**355**	**294**	**364**	**310**	**234**	**209**	96	**2743**

Source: WTO Secretariat, 2005.

2

Calculating Normal Value as a Way of Protection

Some Evidence from Turkish Dumping Investigations

CENGIZ BAHÇEKAPILI AND MURAT ÇOKGEZEN

Introduction

As multilateral trade agreements have restricted the use of conventional trade protection instruments, such as tariffs, quotas, voluntary export restraints etc., the use of other regulatory tools has flourished to fill the protection void. Anti-dumping regulation, one of these regulatory tools, has become one of the most significant barriers to world trade.[1]

Anti-dumping regulations aim to protect local producers from 'unfair' pricing strategies, such as setting two different prices, one at home and the other abroad (price discrimination), or setting unreasonably low price levels (predatory pricing). These strategies are considered 'unfair' by defenders of anti-dumping duties for two main reasons. First, they can only be sustained with the help of a protected home market or government subsidies that give an 'unfair' advantage over international rivals, which, without access to similar compensation mechanisms, are eventually driven out of the market. Thus, these types of pricing behaviours are believed to distort the market mechanism and its economic merits. Second, it is also assumed that with rivals gone, the dumping company would abuse its market power and significantly reduce the general welfare, both of the importing country and globally. Defenders of anti-dumping measures believe that anti-dumping duties both enhance the operation of the

1. Blonigen and Prusa (2003) stress that "...since 1980 GATT/WTO members have filed more complaints under the AD (anti-dumping) statute than under all other trade laws combined, or that more AD duties are now levied in any one year worldwide than were levied in the entire period 1947-1970" (p. 251).

(free trade) market economy and remedy the negative effects of dumping on economies.

Even though the economic justification for anti-dumping may appear quite convincing, many economists are not satisfied with this reasoning. They frequently question and examine the implications of anti-dumping on the welfare of importing countries, global welfare and trade and find countervailing results.[2] However, these discussions are beyond the scope of this chapter. Rather, this chapter concentrates on the problems of anti-dumping applications in practice, with an analysis of the biased calculations of Turkish anti-dumping authorities in favour of domestic producers. Our study reveals that Turkish anti-dumping authorities use discretionary practices during the course of dumping investigation for protective purposes, and also shows that an alternative calculation for dumping margins may give different results than those calculated by the Turkish authorities.

The chapter is organised as follows. The following section discusses methodological problems in the dumping calculations based on the Agreement on Implementation of Article VI of the General Agreement on Tariffs and Trade 1994 (henceforth, the GATT Agreement), as well as the practical difficulties. Section 3 provides empirical evidence for the use of dumping determination as a protective tool by the Turkish authorities. Section 4 reviews confirmed dumping decisions of Turkish authorities using an alternative methodology, and Section 5 concludes the chapter.

Calculating Normal Value as a Way of Protection

Economic theories that provide justification for anti-dumping measures are based on price discrimination and predatory pricing models, in which exporters charge two different prices in two segregated markets (home and abroad) or set a price below costs. However, the GATT Agreement is unable to provide such a clear definition of dumping as is possible in economic theory. The GATT Agreement considers a product as dumped when the export price of the product is less than its normal value. However, the determination of 'normal value' is problematic as anti-dumping law targets two different pricing strategies. In price discrimination the reference price is the sales price in the home market, whereas in predatory pricing it is the cost of production.

2. For a comprehensive survey of these discussions, see Niels (2000).

The preferred method for the determination of normal value by the GATT Agreement is "the comparable price, in the ordinary course of trade, for the like product when destined for consumption in the exporting country"[3] (Home Market Price, HMP). In cases in which "there are no sales of the like product in the ordinary course of trade in the *domestic market* of the exporting country or when, because of the particular market situation or the low volume of the sales in the domestic market of the exporting country, such sales do not permit a proper comparison"[4] then the GATT Agreement recommends two alternative price references for that purpose: the export price to an 'appropriate'[5] third country (Third Market Price, TMP) or the cost of production in the country of origin (Constructed Value, CV).

The above-mentioned rules apply only to market economies. Non-market economies (NME) are subject to a different methodology since all prices, both of exported products as well as the same of the inputs used in production, are controlled by the state. Therefore, neither HMP nor CV data compiled from NME are deemed unreliable. Instead, the input price data obtained from a 'surrogate country', one which is at a similar level of economic development, is used in order to construct a cost price of the exporter in that case.

A dumping investigation authority needs information in order to calculate normal value. Hence the authority sends questionnaires to the interested parties requesting sales and cost information. If an interested party fails to provide accurate and complete information, for whatever reason, the investigation authority may make its final determination "on the basis of the facts available (FA)"[6], which is usually used to punish countries which refrain from cooperation.

Of these five methodologies—HMP, TMP, CV, NME and FA—the HMP and TMP definitions of normal value are based on the price discrimination model, while CV and NME measure below cost pricing. FA can be used for both. Lindsey (1999) shows that only one of these methodologies has any relevance to the detection of market-distorting price discrimination, while none of them measures whether sales are below cost. Lindsey then goes on to examine 141 anti-dumping determinations by the US Commerce Department. He found that only

3. GATT Agreement, Part I, Article 2, Paragraph 2.1.
4. *ibid.*, Paragraph 2.2.
5. *ibid.*, Paragraph 2.2.
6. *ibid.*, Article 6, Paragraph 6.8.

2 of the 107 affirmative determinations had used an appropriate methodology for the determination of dumping. Lindsey concludes that US anti-dumping law fails to distinguish between normal commercial pricing and dumping practices, and in fact ends up punishing normal business practices.

Several other country case studies (Blonigen, 2003; Ikenson, 2005; Niels, 2000; Nielsen and Rutkowski, 2005; Srivats, 2001)[7] indicate that there are several implementation problems related to the calculation of normal value, and that in the presence of these measurement problems several countries applied the anti-dumping laws to favour domestic interests during the course of calculation. Issues regarding the inaccuracies and inadequacies of calculations of normal value under the GATT Agreement in these studies can be classified under four broad categories:

1. *Comparing different prices*: Investigating authorities usually compare individual export prices to a weighted average HMP, or else deduct certain sales costs from the dumper's export price but not from the importing country's home market price. In addition, while calculating these prices, instead of the date on which the material terms of the transactions are established, authorities arbitrarily use the date of the sale invoice, or of the shipment, or the date when a long-term contract is signed.
2. *Comparing different country prices*: If the exporting country is an NME, price data is obtained from a 'surrogate' country, chosen by the investigating authority for the provision of a market price for a proper normal value calculation. In some cases, however, the 'surrogate' country may not be comparable to the NME. Higher prices in the surrogate country may yield higher dumping margins for the exporter. Even if a comparable surrogate country is found, investigators use the available price data differently in each case, mainly to protect domestic producers.
3. *Comparing different product prices*: Price comparisons for dumping margin calculations must be made for identical products. In the absence of an identical product, the 'next most similar' product is used. Determination of the similar product may influence the dumping margins. Sometimes price comparisons are made by

7. See also other chapters in this volume.

using the goods with different qualities. In many cases, applicants (domestic producers) and exporters disagree on the products to be investigated.

4. *Use of unreliable and biased data and calculation techniques*: During the dumping investigations, the authority collects the data from the exporter and other companies in the exporting country. However, respondents' records may not be compatible with the investigating (importing) country's standards, or be not sufficiently detailed for investigating authority's requirements. Given the inadequate data, the investigating authority makes the necessary adjustments to calculate the dumping margins, and these adjustments usually favour producers in the importing country.

For a fair comparison, two prices (ex-factory prices, for example) of the same (or like) product in two countries are needed. Achieving such prices necessitates making some adjustments, which carries the risk of the inclusion of costs not directly associated with the subject product. Investigation authorities make biased price adjustments resulting in an overestimation of subject goods costs and dumping margins.

Another example of bias due to a price adjustment practice open to selective interpretation by the investigation authority is the case of supplier-exporter affiliation. When a supplier is affiliated to the subject exporter, the investigation authority has the right to increase the price of the input, bought from the affiliated supplier, if one of the other benchmarks is higher than the price actually paid, based on the assumption that input prices are subsidised by an affiliated supplier. Such a provision obviously gives the investigation considerable scope for bias.

Finally, the overall dumping margin is calculated by averaging dumping margins of individual cases. However individual negative margins are set equal to zero (zeroing) and thus are not included in average dumping margin estimation. This technique artificially inflates average dumping values.

Anti-Dumping Practices in Turkey

Turkey enacted its first anti-dumping code, the Legislation on Prevention of Unfair Competition in Importation (LPUCI), in 1989. This code, amended in 1999, covers provisions for protection from dumped imports. It was formulated in accordance with the provisions of the Tokyo Round Anti-dumping Code of GATT, which regulated technical and official procedures.

Turkey signed the Final Act of the Uruguay Round and the Marrakesh Agreement establishing the World Trade Organization, and this Act was ratified by the Turkish Grand National Assembly in 1995. In that respect, the WTO Anti-dumping Agreement has the force of law in Turkey, by virtue of the Turkish Constitution. The WTO Anti-dumping Agreement is thus the main reference for the Turkish anti-dumping authority. In practice, it is fully observed by Turkey and in cases of conflict the Agreement has binding precedence over domestic legislation.

In Turkey two separate bodies are involved in anti-dumping proceedings: the Board of Evaluation of Unfair Competition in Importation (henceforth the Board) and the Department of Dumping and Subsidy Investigation (henceforth the Department). The Board is empowered to take decisions for the initiation of investigations, acceptance of undertakings, and termination of investigations or imposition of anti-dumping duties. The Department makes preliminary examinations upon complaint, presents proposals to the Board on whether to initiate an investigation or to take measures, and carries out such investigations.

In recent years, as in many developing countries, there has been an increasing use of anti-dumping rules in Turkey, for protective purposes (Table 2.1). Turkey initiated the fourth highest number of anti-dumping investigations among WTO member countries in 2004 (25, jumping from none in 1996), and imposed an increasing number of new measures each year. While no measures were taken in 1998, the number of measures peaked to 28 in 2003. Currently,[8] there are 28 anti-dumping measures in force in Turkey.

We examined each communiqué reporting the investigation process and the findings and results of each case related to the measures currently in force in Turkey.[9] We found that during the

8. As of 30.4.2006.

9. The list of products subject to anti-dumping duties and related communiqués is prepared by the Turkish Prime Ministry, Under-Secretariat for Foreign Trade, General Directorate for Import, Dumping and Subsidy Investigation Department. This list is available at the official website of the Turkish Republic Prime Ministry, Under-Secretariat for Foreign Trade, at *http://www.dtm.gov.tr/ithalat/english/trade/duties.xls*, (30.04.2006).

Table 2.1

Anti-Dumping Initiations and Measures by Turkey (01/01/1996 – 30/06/2005)

Categories	*1996*	*1997*	*1998*	*1999*	*2000*	*2001*	*2002*	*2003*	*2004*	*Jan.- June 2005*	*Total*
Number of Anti-Dumping Initiations	0	4	1	8	7	15	18	11	25	8	97
Rank in Anti-Dumping Initiations Among WTO Members	-	16	23	10	10	8	6	8	4	5	-
Number of Anti-Dumping Measures	0	0	0	1	8	2	11	28	16	4	81

Source : WTO (2006), Statistics on Anti-dumping, available at *http://www.wto.org/english/tratop_e/adp_e/adp_e.htm* (30.04.2006).

Table 2.2

Objections by Categories Against 28 Turkish Anti-Dumping Measures in Force in 2006 during the Investigation Period

Categories of Objections	*Rejected*	*Approved*	*Total*
Cost Allocations	41	5	46
Product Sampling	15	4	19
Price Adjustment	11	2	13
Market or Non-Market Economy	11	0	11
Profit Adjustment	3	0	3
Country Sampling	5	0	5
Procedure	5	2	7
Others	2	0	2
Total	**93**	**13**	**106**

Source : Turkish Prime Ministry Under-Secretariat for Foreign Trade 2006, The List of Anti-dumping Measures in Force, *http://www.dtm.gov.tr/ithalat/english/trade/duties.xls*, (30.04.2006).

investigations of these measures, accused companies and countries raised a total of 106 objections (Table 2.2). The majority of the objections were in the area of cost allocation, followed by product sampling and price adjustment issues. In 11 of the cases, companies claimed that they were operating under market circumstances and requested not to be assessed according to NME calculation. We classified other objections under the categories profit adjustment, country sampling, procedure and others. Of the 106 objections, only 13 were accepted by the authorities, the rest being rejected for a variety of reasons.

Even a cursory examination shows that most of the objections raised by the exporters were well argued and consistent, and responses to these objections give the impression of discretionary decisions. Probably in many cases, the high cost of carrying relevant discussion further, to the WTO, compared to projected returns, mitigated against exporters taking further steps.

Considering that the objecting parties are also biased, we examined the appropriateness of normal value calculations made by Turkish authorities, in communiqués issued for each Turkish anti-dumping measure in force in 2006 available in the list of products subject to anti-dumping duties, (henceforth the List) issued by Under-Secretariat for Foreign Trade, General Directorate for Import, Dumping and Subsidy Investigation Department. Our findings give numerous clues about biased judgements in calculating normal value. We have compiled arbitrary and biased decisions of the Turkish authorities, derived from communiqués issued, for all the anti-dumping duties imposed in the following three broad categories:

'Appropriate' Third Country

In recent years, dumping and competition from Chinese products in particular has been considered the primary challenge to 'fair' free trade throughout the world. Turkey is no exception to this, and it is therefore Chinese companies, which have been subject to the highest number of investigations by the Turkish anti-dumping authorities. This phenomenon has given rise to an increased use and extended discussion of NME methodology in Turkey. As mentioned above, NME methodology is based on the use of 'appropriate' third country prices for normal value construction when the exporter company comes from a non-market economy. Importing countries have exercised significant discretion in the calculation of normal value for products exported from non-market economies. The legal base for the calculation of normal value for NME is provided by the 7th Article of Regulation on Prevention of Unfair Competition in Importation.[10] According to the Article, the following prices can be used for normal value calculation: the export prices of an 'appropriate' country to third countries, including Turkey; the price of the subject goods in the third country; the 'constructed value' of a similar product in the third country; or, and most interestingly, the market price of or 'constructed value' for similar goods produced in Turkey. Disregarding the other options, it is clear that the application of this last option alone can operate as a protective catchall, insofar as it never allows negative dumping margins since local producers usually have a disadvantage in production costs against the exporters who are subject to investigation for similar product.

As a result of an examination of all communiqués regarding anti-dumping duties currently in practice, we found 34 NME cases. For these cases, the Department sent questionnaires to only 12 'appropriate' countries and received timely responses from just 2. In 16 (almost half) of the cases, input or product prices in Turkey were used for normal value calculations. Obviously, the increasing use of Turkey itself as a third country reduces the reliability of dumping decisions made by the Department.

From the communiqués in the List, we selected six extraordinary cases, which show differing and arbitrary applications of the NME method to similar cases. In each of the following cases a dumping investigation is initiated on (a company from) an NME, and questionnaires are sent to a third country, with no response. Then, there is a lack of uniform treatment to non-responding parties.

In the first case,[11] an investigation to China, Taiwan is chosen as surrogate country and questionnaires are sent to Taiwanese producers. With no response to the questionnaire, normal value was calculated on the basis of the export price of Taiwan to the European Union.[12]

In the second case,[13] the Turkish authority again initiated an investigation against China. Pakistan was chosen as surrogate country.

---

10. Regulation no. 23861, dated 30.10.1999.

11. Communiqué no. 2001/2.

12. A similar method is used for dumping calculation in the following section.

13. Communiqué no. 2002/15.

With no response received for the questionnaire send to Pakistani companies, the Department used the price available in an invoice chosen arbitrarily from an importer of the subject product (pencils, in this case) from Pakistan.

In four other cases[14] without returned questionnaires, the FA rule is applied but no evident explanation recorded for the data, especially the prices, used for calculation.

Like Product

Another major problem we observed in communiqués is linked to the determination of 'like product' for appropriate comparison. The commodities that are subject to foreign trade are classified under Combined Nomenclature (CN) codes. In some investigations, subject products are assessed on the basis of the CN code, but a dumping duty is imposed at the end of the investigation on all the products classified under this CN code.

Products under a particular CN code are differentiated in terms of size, function, quality, etc. The GATT agreement therefore specifies general rules for 'Like Product' determination. According to Article 2.6 in the Anti-dumping Agreement, "like product shall be interpreted to mean a product which is identical, i.e., alike in all respects to the product under consideration, or in the absence of such a product, another product which, although not alike in all respects, has characteristics closely resembling those of the product under consideration." The LPUCI definition of 'like product' is much the same, namely, a "product which has similar characteristics with the product which is subject to dumping or subsidy, or in the absence of such a product, another product which has similar characteristics."

Considering broad range of data under a CN code, an investigation authority should be expected to distinguish a group of products falling under a given code that are similar to the subject goods from the other products falling under the code, and then compare this sub-group of products to the subject goods. For example, under the broad category of apples, an investigation authority would distinguish cooking apples from eating apples, and compare the prices of cooking apples to those of the imports from the subject country.

---

14. Communiqué nos. 2002/15, 2004/15, 2004/19, 2004/24.

The communiqués we examined have many instances in which the like product determined by the Department was questioned by subject country firms. Three such cases are described below. As detailed analyses of each like product dispute require specific knowledge about each subject product, we preferred cases on rather simple consumer goods, discussion about which anyone can easily follow. In the cases described, there is not only a valid question regarding the choice of like product, but also of whether the product is even produced at all in Turkey.

The first case[15] concerns products under the CN code 9105.21, which are battery, accumulator or mains powered wall clocks with plastic or wooden frames, with or without a pendulum, and with or without a melody mechanism. Obviously, a wide range of products falls under this classification. The Department used the product sampling method when comparing domestic and imported products and found evidence of dumping. Then, the Department imposed a duty on all products under the code 9105.21. Actually, the Department is unsure if their sample is really alike. In their report, it is mentioned that imported clocks have a melody mechanism, which is not available in domestic clocks. Despite this difference, they did not change their decision, on the basis that melody has no effect on the function. However, it is clear that existence of a melody mechanism imposes an additional cost on a clock. This does not appear to exemplify the idea of like product as set out by GATT and LPUCI.

The second case concerns rubber bicycle or motorcycle tires and tubes handled in communiqués 2003/6, 2004/22 and 2003/7. In these three investigations domestic producers admitted that they are not producing the type of bicycle tires that are the subject of the investigation, but stated that they would be able to do so with a little additional cost. Two conclusions can be drawn from these reports. First, this is a clear case of a dumping duty being imposed on imports of certain products, which actually are not produced in Turkey. Second, even if it were produced in Turkey it would imply additional cost on local producers. Accordingly, normal value calculation based on a like product, chosen with the criteria mentioned above, would be wrong and unjust.

15. Communiqué no. 2001/5.

Finally, in communiqué 2003/22 an investigation regarding pots and pans is reported. Importers raised objections to the investigation claiming that gold-coloured, steel-framed pot lids are not produced in Turkey. A producer responded to this claim with the assertion that these lids could be produced with a slight change in the mould of another type of pot lid. Again in this case there is no domestic production of the subject goods and production would only be possible with additional cost. In this case, however, there is a further complication as importers raised an additional objection with the claim that the quality of the imported lids was better than the domestic counterparts. Local producers admitted that in the earlier years of domestic production there had occurred some cases of explosion, but defended themselves on the basis that they had overcome this problem by improving production technology and quality control standards. This debate clearly shows that quality differences between domestic and imported products offers another aspect to the interpretation of like product subject to biased interpretation by the anti-dumping authority.

Generalisation

We also found two striking cases more related to the 'interpretation' of calculations, rather than calculations themselves. In the first, a dumping investigation was performed against China and Russian Federation for commodities under CN Codes 7312.10.82, 7312.10.84, 7312.10.86, 7312.10.88 and 7312.10.00, and under communiqué number 2004/4. In this investigation, while comparing normal value and export prices and calculating the dumping margin, a unique representative product was chosen from the 7312.10.82 category for China and from the 7312.10.84 category for the Russian Federation. The final dumping margins calculated by the official authority were 181.5 per cent of the CIF export price (1.65 USD/kg) for China and 89.6 per cent (0.65 USD/kg) for the Russian Federation. Then, using these single calculations, the Department put the measurement against dumping at 0.65 USD/kg for Russian and 1.65 USD/kg for Chinese imported commodities for all the five categories listed above This is obviously an unfair anti-dumping case showing how a bias may be generated by a selective use of sample products in the initial calculations and can be further compounded by its application to a range of categories.

In the second case, under the investigation in Communiqué numbered 2001/2 against China the Department had directed questionnaires to interested parties, only one of which had responded usefully. After examination of the response of this single company, the investigation party felt able to state the following computation: "...the related company's unit price of commodity, which is subject to export, is at the same level as the average export price to Turkey from China." Contrary to this flimsy but nevertheless factual determination, however, Turkish Trade Under-Secretaries concluded the case by issuing the same fixed rate of anti-dumping tax to all Chinese exporter companies of the product. Tellingly perhaps, even the cooperating company did not react against the primary description of dumping under the GATT Agreement, despite having been penalised with unfair, fixed-rate taxes.

Another Non-Perfect Dumping Calculation

Finally, in the light of these inaccuracies and inadequacies, we recalculated dumping margins for the products, which Turkish authorities had deemed dumped and decided to apply duties to. By doing this, we aim to show that dumping margins depend heavily on the methodology and calculation method used for normal value determination.

For this purpose we used a very similar procedure to the TMP methodology, comparing a weighted average home country export price of the subject goods during the investigation period to an export price of the country being investigated. Data for the calculations were compiled from the United Nations Commodity Trade Statistics Database (COMTRADE), a comprehensive database that provides data on export and import prices of a variety of products. In each case, export prices (both from the home country and to the investigating country) corresponding to the CN code of the subject goods available in the List were obtained from this database.

As described in the GATT Agreement, TMP methodology uses an 'appropriate' third country price as proxy for HMP, comparing the third market export price to the export price of the country under investigation. Problems associated with this methodology are discussed in Lindsey (1999). As mentioned above, in practice, costs in an 'appropriate' third country may also be used as a proxy for CV in the home country, an alternative procedure which suffers from the same methodological problems. Another criticism of the selected method may be that the product categories that are used cover not only the subject goods but also other, related goods. However, as mentioned above, 'like products' are frequently used in official investigation processes. Additionally, if duties are imposed on all of the goods covered by the related category, it is more reasonable to determine prices for each category rather than individually. Notwithstanding these weaknesses of the selected method, it is hard to say that it is less perfect than other methodological approaches, especially given the inadequacies and inaccuracies of the other methodologies and calculation techniques. The main reason for choosing TMP, despite the inadequacies, is ease of accessibility of the data.

Our calculations (Table 2.3) show that in 35 out of 87 cases in which Turkish authorities detected dumping and imposed duties, the average world export prices of the exporter are higher than the export prices to Turkey. Importantly, had an alternative methodology such as ours been employed, 'negative' dumping margins would have been found in some of the cases.

Table 2.3

Alternative Dumping Calculation

CN Code	*Exporter Country*	*Export Price to World*	*Export Price to Turkey*	*CN Code*	*Exporter Country*	*Export Price to World*	*Export Price to Turkey*
5503.20	Indonesia	0.74	0.75	5514	China	0.81	0.54
5503.20	Rep. of Korea	0.74	0.80	5514	China	0.80	0.69
5503.20	Chinese-Taipei	0.98	*	5515	China	0.52	0.53
5503.20	India	0.86	0.85	5515	China	0.64	0.39
5503.20	Thailand	0.73	0.80	5516	China	0.44	0.28
5503.20	Belarus	1.06	0.87	5516	China	0.58	0.31
5402.43	Rep. of Korea	0.31	1.55	6301.40	China	5.01	10.99
7307.19	Brazil	2.52	1.14	6301.90	China	4.02	17.08
7307.19	Brazil	2.46	1.10	6001.92	China	2.61	2.40
7307.19	China	0.92	0.86	9609.10	China	2.40	2.21
7307.19	China	0.86	0.72	4011.40	China	3.17	3.11
5402.33	Chinese-Taipei	1.39	1.46	8301.60	China	2.92	2.37
5402.33	Rep. of Korea	1.59	1.66	2905.42	Ukraine	0.88	0.86

Contd. ...

...Contd. ...

CN Code	*Exporter Country*	*Export Price to World*	*Export Price to Turkey*	*CN Code*	*Exporter Country*	*Export Price to World*	*Export Price to Turkey*
5402.33	India	1.74	1.68	2905.42	China	N.A.	N.A
5407	China	0.66	0.45	7010.20	China	1.06	0.78
5407	Malaysia	0.40	0.28	7315.81	China	N.A	N.A
5407	Rep. of Korea	6.82	5.79	7315.82	China	0.70	0.64
5407	Thailand	3.79	2.77	4007.00	Malaysia	1.57	1.85
9613.10	China	0.03	0.03	8302.50	China	1.24	1.30
3904.10	Belgium	0.55	0.54	5605.00	China	4.83	5.60
3904.10	Germany	0.60	0.56	5605.00	India	6.03	4.80
3904.10	Greece	0.59	0.64	5605.00	Rep. of Korea	7.79	7.22
3904.10	Finland	N.A.	N.A.	9607.11	China	0.14	0.12
3904.10	Hungary	0.51	0.50	9607.19	China	0.05	0.04
3904.10	Israel	0.51	0.51	4011.61	China	5.69	10.43
3904.10	Italy	0.60	0.46	4011.62	China	2.20	4.19
3904.10	Netherlands	0.49	0.45	4011.63	China	289.16	109.87
3904.10	Romania	0.45	0.43	4011.69	China	2.75	*
3904.10	USA	0.64	0.37	4011.92	China	2.27	*
4013.20	China	0.41	0.40	4011.93	China	5.42	*
4013.20	Sri Lanka	0.41	0.37	4011.94	China	114.03	1260.33
4013.20	Vietnam	N.A.	N.A.	4011.99	China	8.17	17.11
4011.50	China	1.01	0.86	7315.20	China	1.29	1.10
4011.50	India	1.24	1.28	7408.11	Russian Federation	2.81	2.83
5513	China	0.45	0.30	5801	China	1.26	1.57
5513	China	0.50	0.35	5801	China	4.37	4.39

Source : United Nations Statistics Division (2006), Commodity Trade Statistics Database (COMTRADE), *http://unstats.un.org/unsd/comtrade/dqBasicQuery.aspx*, (30.05.2006).

Note * : No export to Turkey in the year of investigation.

Conclusion

A methodical examination of inquiries and statistics of the WTO indicates that anti-dumping mechanisms are becoming a very important and potentially dangerous virtual device for trade-restriction. Numerous countries are highly active in making use of anti-dumping regulations as a trade-restricting method, and are making increasing efforts to maintain them.

This study contributes to a growing body of research that clearly establishes that the acknowledged methods for factual determination of normal value under the GATT Agreement are extremely problematic and controversial. Furthermore, the GATT Agreement itself and the anti-dumping regulations of individual countries have a wide range of open-ended issues and legally ill-defined grey areas, which allows official authorities to make unfair and biased decisions. Corroborating evidence from Turkish dumping investigations in this chapter is limited to the aspect of normal value calculation, but it would not be very hard to extend the research and extract empirical evidence that raises additional controversial issues from Turkish anti-dumping investigations.

Anti-dumping measures have many gradual implications on local importers; consumers and producers that utilise imported commodities, which are liable to anti-dumping duties. The exporter country and its companies are also major affected parties. A party, which is negatively affected because of unfair anti-dumping practices, may, technically, object to measures and formally ask for an amendment or withdrawal of these measures from the WTO or local authorities. However, affected parties typically hesitate to go forward, for a variety of reasons including bureaucratic obstacles, the material cost of objections and alternative cost of time. This leads to the establishment of unfair measurements as a permanent and commonly applied tool against free trade.

It might be a concrete alternative to reform methods of calculating normal value and describe clearly blurred definitions, thereby taking away from authorities their currently wide-ranging freedom to make subjective calculations and biased decisions about duties to be imposed. Dismantling anti-dumping regulations would be another comprehensive option.

References

Blonigen, B.A. (2003). "Evolving Discretionary Practices of U.S. Anti-dumping Activity", *NBER Working Paper*, No. 9625.

Blonigen, B.A. and T.J. Prusa (2003). "Anti-dumping", in E.K. Choi and J. Harrigan (eds.), *Handbook of International Trade*, Oxford, U.K. and Cambridge, MA, Blackwell Publishers, pp. 251-284.

Ikenson, D. (2005). "Abuse of Discretion: Time to Fix the Administration of the US Anti-dumping Law", *Trade Policy Analysis*, No. 31, Cato Institute Center for Trade Policy Studies.

Lindsey, B. (1999). "The US Anti-Dumping Law: Rhetoric versus Reality", *Trade Policy Analysis*, No. 7, Cato Institute Center for Trade Policy Studies.

Niels, G. (2000). "What is Anti-Dumping Policy Really About", *Journal of Economic Surveys*, 14(4), pp. 467-492.

Nielsen, J.U. and A. Rutkowski (2005). "The EU Anti-dumping Policy Towards Russia and China: Product Quality and the Choice of an Analogue Country", *The World Economy*, Vol. 28, No. 1, pp. 103-136.

Srivats, K.R. (2001). "China, Russia in Government's List of 'Non-Market Economies'", *Business Line* (Financial Daily), June 5, p. 1.

Tharakan, P.K.M. (1999). "Is Anti-Dumping Here to Stay?" *The World Economy*, 22(2), pp. 179-206.

Turkish Prime Ministry Under-Secretariat for Foreign Trade (2006). "The List of Anti-dumping Measures in Force", *http://www.dtm.gov.tr/ithalat/english/trade/duties.xls*.

———. (various dates). "Communiqués for Anti-dumping Measures in Force", *http://www.dtm.gov.tr/ITHALAT/mevzu/haksiz/teblig.htm*.

United Nations Statistics Division (2006). Commodity Trade Statistics Database (COMTRADE), *http://unstats.un.org/unsd/comtrade/dqBasicQuery.aspx*.

WTO (2006). Statistics on Anti-dumping, *http://www.wto.org/english/tratop_e/adp_e/adp_e.htm*.

3

Anti-Dumping Procedures: Lessons for Developing Countries with Special Emphasis on the South African Experience[1]

NICOLA THERON

Introduction

Before the negotiations of the General Agreement on Tariffs and Trade (GATT) Uruguay Round, the favoured barriers to trade used by most countries were tariffs, import quotas, import bans, discretionary permits, etc. Although anti-dumping measures date back as far as the early 1920s when it was discussed by the then League of Nations, this "sophisticated trade instrument" has remained the "tool of protection of the elite" (Vermulst, 1997:5). In 1988 it was estimated that 95 per cent of the 1456 new anti-dumping cases reported since the conclusion of the Tokyo Round Anti-Dumping Code, have been initiated in Australia, Canada, the European Community and the United States (Vermulst and Waer, 1991:6). These four have been the traditional users of anti-dumping measures.

However, after the conclusion of the latest round of multilateral negotiations, traditional barriers to trade such as tariffs are being replaced by measures such as anti-dumping and countervailing duties. Thus, more and more developing countries are also adopting anti-dumping legislation and entering the international arena of anti-dumping investigations. Since the Uruguay Round there have been an explosion of anti-dumping measures worldwide, especially in developing countries. The problem is that the Uruguay Round Anti-Dumping Agreement is a complicated, technical and sometimes

1. A version of the chapter has been presented earlier at the ABAS international conference, Budapest, Hungary, 1998 and is currently available at the webpage of Econex, Cape Town, South Africa at the following link - *http://www.econex.co.za/researcharticles/Nicola_anti-dumping.pdf*. We are thankful to Dr. Nicola Theron for granting us the necessary permission to re-print it.

confusing document, which complicates matters for new users. Often these countries do not have the technical staff to handle these investigations.

Therefore, as anti-dumping seems to become a more and more popular trade instrument, it is necessary to look at the experience of some developing countries that have successfully applied anti-dumping measures in recent years. There are quite a few good examples, Korea for instance has applied its first anti-dumping duty in 1991 and has managed to implement a workable system. South Africa is also a typical case, having in the past relied heavily on the use of formula duties to counteract disruptive competition. In 1993 it had anti-dumping duties on only three products. This changed dramatically and during 1996 South Africa introduced 30 anti-dumping actions, more than any other country in the world (Cohen, 1997). This chapter will look at the lessons that other developing countries can draw from South Africa's experience, while also considering the examples of countries such as Venezuela, Israel, Korea and Turkey.

South Africa

South Africa was one of the founding members of the original GATT treaty that came into being in 1947. Since then, the trade regime in South Africa has changed from a decisively inward looking orientation, to a more outward oriented approach. This is in line with the prescriptions of GATT and specifically with the requirements of the Uruguay Round, which was completed during December 1993. On 2 December 1994 South Africa became a member of the World Trade Organization (WTO), which replaced the GATT. South Africa is becoming more and more outward oriented, moving away from the protectionist regime and import substituting philosophies, which it had followed for decades. This trade liberalisation accompanied the political transformation process as South Africa finally left behind its isolated past.

South Africa has committed itself, in accordance with the agreements reached during the Uruguay Round to the lowering of tariff rates. It is estimated that once the tariff cuts proposed by South Africa in the Uruguay Round have been implemented, the simple average for industrial products will fall to 13.9 per cent (DTI, 1996:64). A recent study by the Industrial Development Corporation

(IDC) predicted an effective rate of protection for the total industry of 14 per cent by 1999 (IDC, 1997: 20). Tariff quotas were terminated on 31 October 1992, import surcharges were abolished by October 1995 and the general export incentive scheme was being phased out during 1997 (GEAR, 1996). Since it has not have taken recourse any longer to some of the traditional barriers to trade, anti-dumping measures have increased at a rapid pace, as mentioned above. By the end of 1996, South Africa had 61 anti-dumping measures in place, placing it alongside countries such as Argentina, with 53 measures and Australia with 64. Other developing countries had less measures in place, for example Brazil (41), Turkey (37) and India (35) could be cited. The United States leads the world by far with 332 actions in force by the end of 1996 (Cohen, 1997).[2]

Procedure

International anti-dumping procedures are ruled by the provisions of Article VI of the General Agreement on Tariffs and Trade (GATT) and specifically by the Agreement on Implementation of Article VI of the GATT 1994. Most countries have based their domestic anti-dumping laws on Article VI. Dumping is normally deemed to be the export of merchandise at a price below its normal value in the home market. All of these concepts are clearly defined in Article VI, but there is ample space for interpretation and therefore these concepts and their application will be dealt with in detail below.

Generally speaking an anti-dumping investigation usually develops along the following lines: a domestic producer makes a request to the relevant authority to initiate an anti-dumping investigation. This body then investigates the practices followed by the foreign producer to determine if the allegation is valid. It uses questionnaires completed by the interested parties to compare the foreign producer's export price to the normal value, i.e., the price in the home market of the exporter. If it is found that the foreign producer is dumping his products, then injury to the domestic industry has to be proved. Lastly the investigating body has to prove a causal link between the alleged dumping and the injury suffered by the domestic industry. Article VI of GATT specifies that dumping investigations shall, except in special circumstances, be concluded within one year, and in no case more

2. Editor's Note: The trend in South Africa's anti-dumping investigations could be seen from Annex A-3.1.

than 18 months after initiation. Anti-dumping measures must expire five years after the date of imposition, unless a determination is made that, in the event of termination of the measures, dumping and injury would be likely to continue to recur.

Some of the more traditional user countries make a division between the determination of dumping and the determination of injury and the calculation of dumping margins. The European Community (EC) has been using separate agencies since 1995 (Vermulst, 1997:8). In the United States, there is also a division. The department of commerce investigates dumping while it is the task of the International Trade Commission to determine whether the domestic industry is being injured by the dumping (White, 1997:118). Korea, a more recent user, also separates the two: the Korean Trade Commission determines whether an investigation is necessary and also determines injury, while the Korean Customs Administration is responsible for the preliminary and final determination of dumping and the collection of the anti-dumping duties (Kim, 1996:105).

Yet, although there seem to be certain merits to the above division of determination of injury and dumping, it would make more sense for developing countries to appoint one investigating body who would run the whole exercise. Especially as there would probably be only a few cases in the beginning and the learning curve would be steeper for the staff involved if they go through the whole exercise and not only a part of it. In Venezuela there is one agency, the anti-dumping and subsidies commission (CASS), which determines both the anti-dumping margins and the injury to the domestic industry. CASS consists of an Executive Body and a Technical Secretariat, the latter being responsible for the day-to-day investigative activity and the preparation of the technical reports (Castro-Bernieri and Levine, 1996:127).

Vermulst (1997:7) mentions three major problems that will face developing countries in the application of anti-dumping laws—a lack of expertise, lack of financial resources, and a lack of manpower.

Therefore, if all the functions are concentrated in one agency, it could minimise these problems. Anti-dumping investigations are multi-disciplinary and therefore require people from different fields. For the day-to-day administration the following disciplines should be represented: law, economics and accountancy. Israeli law makes provision for an advisory committee to administer anti-dumping. It has seven members, three representatives of the public, two staff members of the Ministry of Industry and Trade, one staff member of the Ministry of Finance and a staff member of the Ministry of Agriculture. It specifies that the committee chairman should be a jurist. In South Africa, there is a Board of Tariffs and Trade that is responsible for conducting anti-dumping investigations, with a technical anti-dumping unit within the Department of Trade and Industry.

Interested Parties

Different countries have different specifications as to who might request an investigation. In Japan, applications for protection against dumping may be requested by "Any person who has an interest in an industry in Japan" (Hagiwara *et al.*, 1988:38). The Korean anti-dumping law makes provision for "interested parties of the domestic industry" to submit a petition for the imposition of an anti-dumping duty. But it explains that: "interested parties include producers and associations of producers". Labour unions are specifically excluded (Kim, 1996:106). Under Venezuelan Anti-Dumping Law, only domestic producers of identical or like-products have standing to file petitions requesting the initiation of investigations (Castro-Bernieri and Levine,1996:128). The agreement on Article VI states that an investigation should be initiated "upon a written application by or on behalf of the domestic industry". This is then explained as being:

> By or on behalf of the domestic industry if it is supported by those domestic producers whose collective output constitutes more than 50 per cent of the total production of the like product produced by that portion of the domestic industry expressing either support or opposition to the application. However, no investigation shall be initiated when domestic producers expressly supporting the application account for less than 25 per cent of total production of the like product produced by the domestic industry.

It is important to note here that two different denominators should be used, the first being the portion of the domestic industry either supporting or opposing the application and the second being the total production of the like product.

Vermulst and Komuro (1997:32) say that the most likely areas where new users of anti-dumping laws could err are:

- constructed normal values;
- level of trade, allowable adjustments, averaging;

- injury and causation;
- standing;
- duration and review; and
- motivation.

The following portion of the chapter addresses the issues raised by the industry and some of the other related concerns, looking at the experience of the developing countries.

Constructed Normal Values

According to Article 2 of the Anti-Dumping Agreement a product is being dumped if it is "introduced into the commerce of another country at less than its normal value"(GATT, 1994:145). Therefore the normal value of the product has to be determined and this is done by looking at the comparable price, in the ordinary course of trade, of the product when sold in the exporting country. This information is obtained from the questionnaires completed by the exporters. If this information is readily available, then the calculation of the normal value is simple.

However, Article 2 also provides for a situation where there are no sales of the like product in the ordinary course of trade in the exporting country for some reason. Then the normal value is determined by using the export price of the like product to an appropriate third country or by constructing normal value by calculating the cost of production in the country of origin plus a reasonable amount for administrative, selling and general costs and for profits. The problem usually arises with this last option. Vermulst (1997:18) identifies this method of a constructed normal value as one of the methods used by the traditional user countries to inflate the dumping margin. He suggests that in real dumping situations, the dumping margins will be high enough without any need of inflating them artificially. The 1994 anti-dumping code requires more specific data than before, for the calculation of the constructed normal value: "...the amounts for administrative, selling and general costs and for profits shall be based on actual data pertaining to production and sales in the ordinary course of trade of the like product by the exporter or producer under investigation" (GATT, 1994:146).

The United States seems to be one of the countries that will have to adjust its calculation methods under this new provision of the 1994

Agreement. Most of the criticism against the US Department of Commerce's administration of the anti-dumping law, pertains to the constructed value method. White (1997:119) reports that constructed value is used in the majority of dumping cases. Over two-thirds of the 1987 cases involved cost of production or constructed value methods. Furthermore, it was found that in the USA anti-dumping determinations are made in 89 per cent of the cases in which constructed value is used; which is a greater percentage than in cases where home-market (82 per cent) or third country prices (32 per cent) are used. This would confirm a definite bias towards determination of dumping when the constructed value method is used.

During 1996 and 1997, South Africa has completed 13 investigations where the basis for determination of the normal value has been reported. Of these, 7 used the home market price, 3 the constructed value method and in 3 cases a combination of the home market and constructed values was used. All these three cases dealt with the export of circuit breakers to South Africa, originating in France, Japan and Spain and imported from France, Italy, Switzerland and Japan. The reason why a combination was used, was that some of the circuit breakers (NA 100) imported from France by a company called Groupe Schneider were specifically developed for use in South Africa and therefore not sold in Groupe Schneider's domestic market or anywhere else. For the other circuit breakers, normal values could be determined by looking at the price for which they were sold in the French domestic market. The normal value of the various products not sold in France was determined with reference to cost build-ups, in accordance with Article 2.2.1 of the Agreement. For the products that were sold in France, the normal value was determined on the basis of domestic sales less adjustment for general, selling and administrative costs. A combination of methods was also used for circuit breakers from Japan, as there were significant differences between the product destined for the home market and those exported to South Africa. Hydraulic-magnetic products were exported to South Africa while thermal-magnetic breakers were sold in Japan.

South Africa used in most cases the home market price, only in a few cases was a constructed value calculated and sometimes a combination of the two methods was used. This is reassuring, as the abuse of the constructed value method might indicate unnecessary protection, based on higher dumping duties.

In order to calculate the anti-dumping duty, the export price or dumped price must be compared to the normal value and if the export price is less than the normal value, this will prove dumping. The determination of the export price is not as controversial as that of the constructed normal value. The dumping (or export) price is simply the price really paid for the exported good. Article 2.3 of the Agreement makes provision for a constructed export price, if there is an association or an agreement of such a nature between the exporter and the importer or a third party, which makes the export price unreliable. In such a case the price may be determined on the basis of the price at which the imported products are first resold to an independent buyer, or if not resold in the condition as imported, then on such reasonable basis as the authorities may determine. The usual formula is:

$$\text{Dumping Rate} = \left(\frac{\text{Adjusted Normal Value} - \text{Adjusted Export Price}}{\text{Adjusted Export Price}}\right) \times 100$$

Another problem arises when the weighted-average of the normal values is compared to the dumping price of a specific transaction. In the European Community dumping margins used to be established by comparing the normal value which is the weighted-average of such values for the investigation period, and the export price which was determined on a transaction-by-transaction basis (Kim, 1996:117). After much criticism, this issue was discussed in the Uruguay Round negotiations and the 1994 Agreement (Article 2.4.2) now specifies that: "...margins of dumping...be established on the basis of a comparison of a weighted average normal value with the weighted average of prices of all comparable export transactions or by a comparison of normal value and export prices on a transaction-by-transaction basis". This provision will also necessitate a change in United States procedures, as USA practice had been to compare individual export prices to weighted average normal value. Palmeter (1996:47) found that this method is inherently biased in proving dumping. The Korean practice is to calculate a separate dumping duty for each company, if sufficient data is available. Otherwise a single dumping rate for all exporters from a given country is determined (Kim, 1996:117).

South Africa also follows the practice of calculating individual dumping margins for each exporter. Only in a few isolated cases were dumping margins calculated for the entire industry. In a recent investigation of the dumping of glazed and unglazed ceramic tiles from Italy, five exporters were selected. As there were approximately 200 exporters it was administratively impossible to calculate margins for each. The five that were chosen exported the biggest volumes to South Africa. For each of these, individual dumping margins were calculated. Three companies had negative dumping margins and were therefore exempted. The weighted average duties of the other two were used to calculate the general dumping duty applicable to all other Italian exporters whose export price was beneath a certain benchmark price. Thus developing countries, implementing anti-dumping laws, should be careful not to disregard the provisions of Article 2.4.2 by comparing weighted average normal values with individual export prices.

Material Injury

In order to levy an anti-dumping duty, it is not enough only proving that dumping has occurred. Article 3 of the Agreement requires that injury to the domestic industry also have to be proved. During the 1967 Kennedy Round, the anti-dumping code was made more specific, requiring that a country has to show: "that the dumped imports are demonstrably the principle cause of material injury". This provision was vehemently opposed by the United States, who argued that it placed a heavy burden of proof on the authorities to prove 'material injury' rather than simply injury. However, during the Tokyo Round (late 1970s), the 'principle cause' provision disappeared, but 'material injury' remained, although reduced to a footnote (Palmeter, 1996:44). But it seems that through the years (although still only in a footnote in the 1994 Agreement), injury has come to mean material injury. It is the phrase used in the national anti-dumping laws of New Zealand, Turkey and Japan, to name a few. South Africa also uses this term in its anti-dumping law as well as in its anti-dumping reports.

To prove the existence of material injury, the GATT Agreement specifies certain criteria, which should be considered. The primary criteria are the volume of the dumped imports and their effect on prices in the domestic market for like products and the consequent impact of these imports on the domestic producers. With regard to the effect on prices, consideration should be given to price undercutting, price suppression and price depression. But quite a few other criteria are also listed: actual and potential decline in sales, profits, output, market share, productivity, utilisation of capacity, etc. But it is stated that: "The list is not exhaustive, nor can several of these factors necessarily give decisive guidance"(GATT, 1994).

Most countries have copied this list in their domestic anti-dumping laws; some have simplified it, naming only a few criteria. The important point here is that "A determination of injury ...shall be based on positive evidence..."(Article 3.1). Facts and figures have to be given for criteria such as increases in import volumes, price undercutting, declines in profits, etc. Therefore, it is advisable for newcomers to the anti-dumping arena to limit their investigations to the more easily quantifiable criteria. South Africa has also followed this approach, usually limiting their investigation to the effect on import volumes, domestic prices, sales, profits, production and production utilisation, market share and inventories. In some cases the effect on employment was also considered, if the data was available.

Injury Margins and the Lesser Duty Rule

Article 9 of the Agreement states that: "It is desirable...that the duty be less than the margin if such lesser duty would be adequate to remove the injury to the domestic industry." This provision is not mandatory and the Agreement does not specify how these "lesser duties" should be calculated. Therefore, there are relatively few countries that implement this lesser duty rule. The EC has the practice of routinely calculating two separate duties, an injury margin and a dumping margin. The lower of the two is then used as the punitive duty. The United States and Canada on the other hand are examples of countries that do not calculate injury margins; they use the dumping margin to determine the dumping duty (Vermulst, 1997:19).

If one looks at the methodology of the EC in calculating injury margins, it appears to be rather complicated. As the provision of Article 9 is not mandatory, it would probably be simpler for developing countries to follow the example of the United States and Canada and calculate only a dumping margin, using this as the basis for the dumping duty. Korea is one of the newcomers to the anti-dumping field, which implements the lesser duty rule. Korea also uses a rather complicated method; their use of the lesser duty rule is based on the concept of proper profit. Average profits for different industries (as calculated by the Bank of Korea), is used to determine 'proper profit' and the duty necessary to ensure this. This calculation has not proved satisfactory as the duty based on this method was higher in some cases than the duty based on the dumping margin, e.g., in certain ball-bearings from Thailand and phosphoric acid from the People's Republic of China (Kim, 1996:109).

South Africa uses the lesser duty rule in almost all of their investigations. In the case of circuit-breakers originating in France, Italy, Spain and Japan, it is stated that:

> ... the Board felt that in the light of the extremely high dumping margin of products exported from Bticino, that imposing the anti-dumping duty at the dumping margin, would be punitive and would price their products out of the market, rather than levying the playing field, as was the intended result of the imposition of a final anti-dumping duty (BTT, 1997b:46).

In another case, involving insecticide containing aldicarb originating and imported from the United States of America, there was a substantial difference between the dumping margin (99.3%) and the final duty based on the lesser duty rule (11.5%). Both are expressed as a percentage of the export price. South Africa does not use the same complicated methods as the EC. In the aldicarb case, the duty was based on a calculation of the price disadvantage (BTT, 1997a). In glazed and unglazed ceramic tiles originating and imported from Italy, the Board explains its stance in the preliminary determination: "The Board considered that the provisional payment should be the lesser of the margin of dumping and the price disadvantage, as this could be considered to remove the injury to the domestic industry" (BTT, 1998:52). Thus the practice is to calculate both the price disadvantage and the dumping margin. As illustrated in the aldicarb case the duty based on the price disadvantage is usually lower than the dumping margin and deemed by the BTT in most cases to be sufficient to remove injury or to "level the playing field". Therefore, for developing countries who do not want to use the complicated methods of the EC, it might be advisable to follow the South African example and calculate the price disadvantage and use this as a basis for the application of the lesser duty rule.

Causation

For dumping to be determined all three requirements have to be fulfilled, dumping has to be proved as well as injury and causation, i.e., it needs to be proved that it was the dumping that caused the injury to the domestic industry. Therefore, all other factors that might have caused the injury have to be isolated and investigated separately. Article 3.5 of the Agreement explains: "Factors which may be relevant in this respect include *inter alia,* the volume and prices of imports not sold at dumping prices, contraction in demand or changes in the patterns of consumption, trade restrictive practices of and competition between the foreign and domestic producers, developments in technology and the export performance and productivity of the domestic industry."

Some countries (e.g. New Zealand and Turkey) do not distinguish in their national anti-dumping laws clearly between determination of injury and proving a causal link, although they also investigate the factors that would prove causality. Japan (Hagiwara *et al.,* 1988:43) and Korea (Kim, 1996:125) analyse material injury and causation separately. Although there is a considerable overlap between the two, it makes more sense to separate the two. Vermulst (1997:19) also supports this: "It seems best that importing country authorities follow a two-step approach...it should first be established whether the domestic industry has been materially injured...then be determined whether the material injury is caused by the dumped imports." South Africa also separates these two factors in all their investigations. South African domestic laws also name a few other factors that might indicate causation: political factors, state of the economy, marketing and finance. Therefore, broadly speaking, determining causation requires a wider look at macro-economic indicators, than proving injury, which considers micro-economic indicators pertaining to a specific industry.

National Interest

The 1994 WTO Anti-dumping Agreement does not include a national interest clause. If dumping, injury and causation are proved, then an anti-dumping duty is levied. In the United States, for example, the imposition of anti-dumping duties is mandatory once dumping and resulting injury are found (Vermulst, 1997:20). The main exception here is the EC. Apart from proving dumping and injury, EC law specifies that anti-dumping measures may only be imposed if they are shown to be in the interest of the importing country.

The community interest clause was reinforced and broadened in the 1995 Basic Regulation of the EC. This new community interest provision has since taken on new meaning when it became a serious issue in case of unbleached (grey) cotton fabrics import from China, Egypt, India, Indonesia, Pakistan and Turkey. Heavy opposition to imposition of provisional duties came from the downstream industry. The EC provision gives wider powers to consumers, traders, importers, upstream suppliers and downstream users (Vermulst and Driessen, 1997:155).

The question here is whether developing countries should add such a national interest clause to their anti-dumping laws, as this is not required by the 1994 Agreement. From the experience of those that have adopted such a clause, it would seem that it is not as often used as one might expect. The Korean Anti-Dumping law has as a third requirement (apart from dumping and material injury), the necessity to protect the domestic industry must be proved. However, in practice, the Korean government does not review this requirement separately in its determinations. If dumping and injury are proved, that is deemed to be sufficient to impose an anti-dumping duty (Kim, 1996:126).

Vermulst (1997:20) recommends that developing countries should adopt a national interest provision, as it could offer: "a safety valve if anti-dumping action, for whatever reason, seems undesirable". He foresees that some developing countries might need such a provision if they do not want to impose a duty. South Africa does not have a national interest clause in their domestic anti-dumping laws. They do consider the impact of the duty on the domestic industry when injury is determined, but no provision is made for a broader definition of interested parties, to include consumers and downstream users.

Confidentiality

Another problem that new users of anti-dumping laws may face is how to handle the sensitive nature of some of the information used in anti-dumping procedures. The United States and Canada have a rather complicated (but efficient) system, whereby confidential information, submitted by one party, can be accessed by the attorneys of the other parties. The attorneys are not allowed to disclose this information to their clients, but they may use it to double-check the correctness of the information and the use thereof.

But for developing countries it might be far better to adopt the EC system, whereby interested parties have to submit a non-confidential version of every confidential document (Vermulst, 1997:14). The EC is strict about this rule and in case of unbleached (grey) cotton fabrics import from China, Egypt, India, Indonesia, Pakistan and Turkey, the Commission used only the information from 100 questionnaires from an approximate 200 submitted, because the rest did not have the prescribed non-confidential summary attached (Vermulst and Driessen, 1997:154). How should one determine whether information should be considered as confidential or not? Venezuela asks the following questions: "Would a competitor gain an advantage based on access to this information? Would access to this information have a prejudicial effect on its provider or on a third party? Is the information provided otherwise generally available?" (Castro-Bernieri *et al.*, 1996:130).

South Africa also uses the EC practice; interested parties are required to submit a non-confidential version of all confidential information. This is easily done by using a base year; the first year of data covered is used as the base year. This system seems to be more appropriate for developing countries, as it is easier to administer and chances of confidential information being leaked are minimised.

Price Undertakings

Article 8 of the Agreement makes provision for proceedings to be suspended or terminated without imposing an anti-dumping duty, if the exporters concerned make satisfactory voluntary undertakings to revise its prices or to cease exports at dumped prices. Undertakings cannot be accepted, before a preliminary determination of dumping and injury has been made. Under Korean law, either the exporter or the Korean anti-dumping authority may propose an undertaking. Although their law makes provision for either a price revision or a decrease or cessation of exports, in practice it was the latter method that was used as an undertaking. The same applied for the EC, where anti-dumping proceedings were typically terminated through voluntary restraint arrangements. Japan also used this provision to terminate some of its investigations, e.g., Korean Cotton Yarn and Norwegian-French ferrosilicon (both terminated during 1984) (Hagiwara *et al.*, 1988:49).

Therefore it seems that the more popular of the undertakings was the export restraint undertaking. However, with the conclusion of the Uruguay Round, any measures on exports, such as voluntary export restraints are prohibited (Kim, 1996:108). Developing countries implementing anti-dumping laws should be careful not to step outside the boundaries of the GATT 1994.

Anti-Circumvention

As anti-dumping measures are becoming increasingly popular, so are methods to circumvent it. Exporters and importers will increasingly be looking for new means of circumvention. The Anti-Dumping Agreement however, contains no provisions regarding permitted measures against circumvention. Both the European Community and the United States were hopeful that such measures might be adopted during the Uruguay Round. Palmeter (1996:65) believes that their failure to obtain this: "... was perhaps their major significant set-back in the anti-dumping negotiations." Both the EC and the United States, as well as a number of other countries have resorted to unilateral anti-circumvention measures.

The EC has adopted a detailed anti-circumvention provision in their 1994 basic regulation. Assembly remains the principal form of circumvention. The EC has broadened their anti-circumvention provision to include third-country assembly. Another strict requirement is the so-called value-of parts test, which they set at 60 per cent. Circumvention will be proved if the imported parts constitute 60 per cent or more of the total value of the parts of the assembled product. But if the value added to the imported parts exceeds 25 per cent of the manufacturing costs, then it will not be considered circumvention. The EC has initiated a few proceedings under this new provision (Vermulst and Driessen, 1997:147).

It seems that presently, anti-circumvention is the privileged domain of the more experienced anti-dumping users, in particular the EC. Circumvention remains a controversial issue and at Marrakesh it was decided that the Committee on Anti-Dumping Practices should work on uniform rules that could be added to the Agreement. Therefore, for the moment it might be wise for developing countries to accept the advice of Vermulst (1997:21): "...developing countries might find it in their interest to get experience with 'regular' anti-dumping investigations before embarking upon anti-circumvention investigations."

Conclusion

The increase in anti-dumping investigations over the last years since the conclusion of the Uruguay Round, seem to confirm their increasing importance as the trade-restrictive instruments of choice. Since 1980, 2000 new cases have been initiated by OECD countries (Hoekman and Mavroidis, 1996:27). Developing countries are also increasingly adopting anti-dumping laws. From the experience of some developing countries, which have successfully implemented anti-dumping laws, it is clear that these laws should be as close as possible to Article VI of the GATT, but that they should preferably be a simplified version. South Africa has also followed this approach, adopting a simplified version of the GATT Anti-Dumping Agreement. Developing countries must be careful not to step outside of the GATT boundaries and should give special attention to the problem areas discussed above, such as constructed normal values, material injury, causation, price undertakings, confidentiality, etc.

The main problem at present with the increase in anti-dumping investigations is that this could be a form of neo-protectionism. The US International Trade Commission has published a report in 1996 on US anti-dumping measures, in which they used a cost-benefit analysis to evaluate the impact of such measures. It was estimated that the costs to the US economy far outweighed the benefits that US producers derived from anti-dumping relief (Bronckers, 1996:18).

Therefore, in the future it will be necessary for policy-makers to discipline this trade instrument. This could take the form of more comprehensive anti-circumvention measures prescribed by the WTO. For developing countries, this means that they should take care from the beginning that anti-dumping measures do not become a protection tool for domestic producers.

References

Blumberg, L. (1995). "South Africa and the Uruguay Round", *Development Southern Africa*, October, Vol. 12(5), pp. 769-775.

Board on Tariffs and Trade (1997a). "Investigation into the Alleged Dumping of an Insecticide Containing Aldicarb Originating in and Imported from the United States of America (USA): Final determination", *Report No. 3789*, Pretoria.

———. (1997b). "Investigation into the Alleged Dumping of Industrial Circuit-breakers Originating in France, Italy, Spain and Japan and imported from France, Italy, Switzerland and Japan: Final Determination", *Report No. 3781*, Pretoria.

———. (1997c). "Investigation into the Alleged Dumping of Penicillin, and More Specifically Ampicillin and Amoxicillin 250 mg and 500 mg Penicillin Capsules, Originating in India and Imported from Ranbaxy Laboratories Limited, India: Final Determination", *Report No. 3799*, Pretoria.

———. (1998a). "Investigation into the Alleged Dumping of Glazed and Unglazed Ceramic Tiles Originating and Imported from Italy: Preliminary Determination", *Report No. 3811*, Pretoria.

———. (1998b). "Investigation into the Alleged Dumping of Uncoated Woodfree Paper in Reels and Sheets, Originating in and/or Imported from Brazil, Indonesia, Poland and Sweden: Final Determination", *Report No. 3824*, Pretoria.

Bronckers, C.E.J. (1996). "Rehabilitating Anti-dumping and Other Trade Remedies through Cost-Benefit Analyses", *Journal of World Trade*, April, Vol. 30(2), pp. 5-39.

Castro-Bernieri, J. and P.A. Levine (1996). "The Venezuelan Anti-dumping and Countervailing Duties Regime", *Journal of World Trade*, February, Vol. 30(1), pp. 125-143.

Cohen, T. (1997). "SA Most Active in Introducing Anti-dumping Rules", Business Day, (Online) available at: *http://www.bday.co.za/97/1117/news/news4.htm*

GEAR (Growth Employment and Redistribution) (1996). *A Macro-economic Strategy*, Government Printers, Pretoria, Available online: *http://www.polity.org.za/html/govdocs/policy/growth.html?rebookmark=1*.

Hagelstam, J. (1991). "Some Shortcomings of International Anti-Dumping Provisions", *Journal of World Trade*, October, Vol. 25(5), pp. 99-110.

Hagiwara, S, Y. Noguchi and K. Masui (1988). "Anti-Dumping Laws in Japan", *Journal of World Trade*, August, Vol. 22(4), pp. 35-50.

Hoekman, M. and C. Mavroidis (1996). "Dumping, Anti-dumping and Antitrust", *Journal of World Trade*, February, Vol. 30(1), pp. 27-53.

IDC (Industrial Development Corporation) (1997). *The Effective Protection Rate and Anti-Export Bias*, Sandton, IDC.

Kim, H.J. (1996). "The Korean Anti-Dumping System", *Journal of World Trade*, April, Vol. 30(2), pp. 101-133.

Palmeter, D. (1996). "A Commentary on the WTO Anti-Dumping Code", *Journal of World Trade*, August, Vol. 30(4), pp. 43-71.

Vermulst, E. (1997). "Adopting and Implementing Anti-Dumping Laws", *Journal of World Trade*, April, Vol. 31(2), pp. 5-25.

Vermulst, E. and B. Driessen (1997). "New Battle Lines in the Anti-Dumping War", *Journal of World Trade*, June, Vol. 31(3), pp. 135-159.

Vermulst, E. and N. Komuro (1997). "Anti-Dumping Disputes in the GATT/WTO", *Journal of World Trade*, February, Vol. 31(1), pp. 5-45.

Vermulst, E. and P. Waer (1991). "The Calculation of Injury Margins in EC Anti-dumping Proceedings", *Journal of World Trade*, December, Vol. 25(6), pp. 5-43.

White, J.J. (1997). "A Test of Consistency in the Administration of US Anti-dumping Law", *Journal of World Trade*, August, Vol. 31(4), pp. 117-129.

WTO (1994). "Agreement on the Implementation of Article VI of the General Agreement on Tariffs and Trade".

———. (1995a). "Semi-Annual Report Under Article 16.4 of the Agreement: South Africa".

———. (1995b). "Minimum Information to be Provided under Article 16.4 of the Agreement in the Reports of All Preliminary or Final Anti-dumping Actions".

———. (1995c). "Notification of Laws and Regulations under Articles 18.5 and 32.6 of the Agreements: New Zealand".

———. (1995d). "Notification of Laws and Regulations under Articles 18.5 and 32.6 of the Agreements: South Africa".

———. (1996a). "Semi-Annual Report Under Article 16.4 of the Agreement: South Africa".

———. (1996b). "Notification of Laws and Regulations under Articles 18.5 and 32.6 of the Agreements: Kenya".

———. (1997). "Semi-Annual Report under Article 16.4 of the Agreement: South Africa".

Annexure A-3.1

Anti-Dumping Investigations by South Africa (year-wise)

Period	*Initiations*	*Provisional Measures*	*Definitive Duties*	*Price Under-takings*	*Measures in Force on the End Date*
1 January 1995 – 31 December 1995	18	9	2	0	15
1 January 1996 – 31 December 1996	50	9	8	0	31
1 January 1997 – 31 December 1997	23	17	18	0	43
1 January 1998 – 31 December 1998	41	33	12	0	57
1 January 1999 – 30 June 1999	7	9	22	0	86
1 July 1999 – 30 June 2000	11	9	16	0	104
1 July 2000 – 30 June 2001	20	9	12	0	109
1 July 2001 – 30 June 2002	2	18	8	0	98
1 July 2002 – 30 June 2003	5	1	8	0	96
1 July 2003 – 30 June 2004	10	6	2	0	84

Source: WTO *Annual Report* (various issues).

4

The Growing Problem of Intra-Developing Country Anti-Dumping Actions in World Trade

KOFI OTENG KUFUOR

Introduction

The Members of the World Trade Organization (WTO)[1] launched the Doha Development Round of trade talks with the specific intention of lowering barriers to trade in the interests of the Developing Country (DC) Members of the WTO.[2] The Ministerial Declaration stated that open global markets were important for economic development and poverty alleviation. The DCs in particular, the Declaration stated, stood to enhance the welfare of their citizens if the multilateral trading system functioned in their interests.[3] The significance of market access for the DCs also lies in the point repeatedly stressed by them that the markets for their exports are closed off as a result of barriers imposed mainly by developed country members of the WTO. This import of market access for the DCs is reinforced by the fact that they are no longer hostile to the idea of participating in the world trading system. They have now come to admit that open markets will enhance their economic growth and development.[4]

---

1. Agreement Establishing the World Trade Organization, available at *http://www.wto.org/English/docs_e/legal_e/04-wto.pdf*.
2. WTO Doha Ministerial 2001: Ministerial Declaration *http://www.wto.org/English/thewto_e/minist_e/min01/mindecl_e.htm*.
3. *ibid.*, para.2.
4. This change is a consequence of the economic mismanagement by the DCs, the obvious success of the NICs, policy advice from the World Bank and IMF, and the influence of research efforts by the academic community. For the benefits of an open trading system for DCs, see the following: D. Ingco, Merlinda (1997). "Has Agricultural Trade Liberalization Improved Welfare in the Least-Developed Countries? Yes," *World Bank Policy Research Working Paper 1748*, The World Bank: Washington DC; Erzan, Refik (1989). "Would General Trade Liberalization in Developing Countries Expand South-South Trade?" (1989). *World Bank Policy Research Working Paper 319*, The World Bank, Washington DC; and Krueger, Anne O. (1998). "Why Trade Liberalisation is Good for Growth", 108 *Economic Journal* No. 450, p. 1513.

However, a particular problem that the DCs face is that of anti-dumping actions against their exports. Even though there is a recent downward trend in initiation of anti-dumping investigations,[5] this form of trade protection still remains a serious dilemma for the DCs in particular in that anti-dumping actions generally account for a decline of their export volumes.[6] What compounds this development is that while some scholars and policy-makers see dumping as ordinary business activity, other proponents of the multilateral trading system see anti-dumping actions as crucial to maintaining "the delicate balance" between the goal of trade liberalisation and national political and economic interests.[7] Thus there is the distinct possibility that enthusiasm for anti-dumping will remain a marked trait of the multilateral trading system irrespective of the harm this practice causes to DC exports.

The overall concern with dumping and the use of anti-dumping actions has led to reform of GATT/WTO rules on anti-dumping being a major feature of trade talks since the Kennedy Round.[8] Not surprisingly therefore, the Doha Ministerial Declaration noted that there was the increasing application of anti-dumping measures and thus reform of the trading system should, according to the Declaration, include the clarification and improvement of trade distorting practices such as anti-dumping actions.[9]

The role of DCs in the context of the multilateral anti-dumping system has been somewhat mixed. The general consensus is that the DCs had very little role to play in this regard. However, this sweeping

---

5. *WTO: 2006 Press Releases WTO Secretariat reports further declines in both new anti-dumping investigations and new final anti-dumping measures* available at *http://www.wto.org/english/news_e/pres06_pr441_ehtm.*

6. A number of studies support this assertion: Neufeld Inge Nora (2001). "Anti-Dumping and Countervailing Procedures – Use or Abuse? Implications for Developing Countries", United Nations Conference on *Trade and Development: Policy Issues in International Trade and Commodities Study Series* No.9, United Nations, Geneva, Switzerland; Cuyvers Ludo and Michel Dumont (2004). "The Impact of Anti-dumping Measures of the EU Against ASEAN Countries on Trade Flows", Centre for ASEAN Studies *Discussion Paper* No.45 available at *http://143.129.203.3/cas/PDF/CAS45.pdf.*

7. Wolff Alan Wm. (1995). "Role of the Anti-dumping Laws", p. 4,, available at *http://www.dbtrade.com/publications/18192w.pdf*. Wolff sees anti-dumping laws as vital for reducing friction arising out of competition between economies with fundamentally different structures. In the absence of effective remedies against dumping, political support for the alternative to internationally-agreed anti-dumping rules is an uncontrolled *ad hoc* regime of tariffs, quotas and non-tariff barriers-trade wars.

8. The Kennedy Round resulted in the first GATT Anti-Dumping Agreement.

9. See Doha Ministerial Declaration, *supra*, para 28.

assumption is rebuttable when the pattern of DC activity is closely scrutinised. There is some evidence to support DC awareness of the body of global anti-dumping rules and their subsequent impact on the shaping of these rules going back to the days of the General Agreement on Tariffs and Trade (GATT). Thus the DCs' role in further development and direction of the WTO anti-dumping system is really just a logical step along a path they have embarked on since they began to join the multilateral trading system.[10]

A recent further evolution of the DCs engagement with the WTO anti-dumping system is that the DCs are beginning to target each other with anti-dumping investigations. Thus, the purpose of this chapter is to examine a number of issues in this regard in the hope that it can make a contribution to any debate on this emerging problem of intra-DC anti-dumping actions. Part II examines factors behind the increasing tendency of the DCs to rely on anti-dumping actions as a form of trade protection. Part III discusses the importance of lessening intra-DC anti-dumping conflicts. Part IV, the conclusion, explores measures that can be adopted by DCs to lessen the likelihood of continued intra-DC anti-dumping actions.

Emergence of DCs as Active Users of Anti-Dumping Actions

The facts indicate that in the early years of the multilateral trading system anti-dumping actions were largely utilised by the United States, Australia, Canada, New Zealand and the European Communities.[11] However, although the DCs hardly initiated anti-dumping complaints during this period, they were the main targets of anti-dumping actions.[12] There, however has been a change in anti-dumping initiations and as of 2005, the DCs had overtaken the traditional users. Over a 10-year period, India has emerged as the leading initiator of anti-dumping investigations with 425 initiations.

10. This is the argument I have advanced in Kufuor Kofi Oteng (1998). "The Developing Countries and the Shaping of GATT/WTO Anti-dumping Law", 32 *Journal of World Trade* No.6 (1998), p.167; and Kufuor Kofi Oteng (2004). *World Trade Governance and Developing Countries: The GATT/WTO Code Committee System*, Blackwell (for the Royal Institute of International Affairs), London.

11. Prusa, Thomas J. (1999). "On the Spread and Impact of Anti-dumping", *National Bureau of Economic Research Working Paper* 7404, pp.5-6, available at *http://ies.fsv.cuni.cz/storage//sylab30_antidumping.pdf*.

12. Messerlin, Patrick (1988). "Anti-dumping Laws and Developing Countries", *Policy Research Working Paper* No.16, The World Bank, Washington DC, p.5.

Argentina and South Africa are 4th and 5th with 204 and 197 initiations respectively, whilst New Zealand, a past anti-dumping enthusiast has fallen, cumulatively, to 16th position.[13]

A consequence of this DC embrace of anti-dumping is that they are engaged in an anti-dumping war amongst themselves. People's Republic of China (PRC), the biggest target in anti-dumping actions by all the members of the WTO was the subject of 86 anti-dumping investigations by India and 47 by Brazil making it the prime target for these two members. In all of the 469 times that PR China was targeted over 1995-2005, 314 of these actions have been initiated by other DCs. The Republic of Korea has faced 218 anti-dumping investigations of which 105 have been launched by other DCs, Brazil faced 65 initiations from other DCs out of the overall initiations made 84 times, whilst Chinese Taipei faced initiations from other DCs 101 times out of the 160 initiations made against it from 1995 to 2005.[14]

The picture is no different when it comes to positive anti-dumping measures imposed by the DCs. The five DCs that had the highest number of anti-dumping measures imposed against them were, respectively, PR China (338), Republic of Korea (127), Chinese Taipei (99), Brazil (64) and India and Indonesia (63 each). Of these the final measures imposed were, PR China (228), Republic of Korea (76), Chinese Taipei (69), Brazil (50), India (34) and Indonesia (39).[15]

It is thus obvious that what was once seen by the DCs as the tool of supposedly insensitive and perfidious policy-makers of the developed world is gradually turning into an instrument to be used enthusiastically by DCs themselves. The question then is what accounts for this development? Before analysing the cause of the growing intra-DC anti-dumping actions, however, we should note here that intra-DC trade conflicts are not new. Rather the DCs have always shielded their economies from threats posed by other DC exports.[16]

---

13. AD Initiations by Reporting Member from: 01/01/95 to 31/12/05, available at *http://www.wto.org/english/tratop_e/adp_stattab2_e.pdf*.

14. AD Initiations: *Reporting Member* vs. *Exporting Country* from: 01.01/95 to 31/12/05, available at *http://www.wto.org/english/tratop_e/adp/_stattab3_e.pdf*.

15. AD Measures: *Reporting Member* vs. *Exporting Country* from: 01/01/95 to 31/12/05, available at *http://www.wto.org/english/tratop_e/adp_e/adp_stattab8_e.pdf~*.

16. Erzan, Refik (1989). "Would General Trade liberalization in Developing Countries Expand South-South Trade?" *Policy Research Working Paper* No.319, World Bank, Washington DC; Erzan, Refik and Alexander Yeats (1990). "Tariff Valuation Bases and Trade Among Developing Countries: Do Developing Countries Discriminate Against their Own Trade?" *Policy Research Working Paper* No.371, The World Bank, Washington DC.

However, anti-dumping actions were not employed that frequently. This is probably because other protectionist tools such as import licences and reference prices provided a more convenient form of shelter from foreign competition.

One probable explanation for the rise in intra-DC anti-dumping actions is the general move by the DC economies from command type economies towards greater economic liberalism. In the 1980s the economies of almost all DCs imploded, ruined by general economic mismanagement. This economic crisis resulted in policy reform under the direction of the Bretton Woods institutions. One major consequence of this was trade liberalisation. Thus, hitherto protectionist DC economies that had closed off their markets arguing, *inter alia,* the need to protect infant industries from a malignant international economic system were now converted to the principles of the free market. As a result of this change, their economies are now open to relatively easier penetration by goods from the advanced countries as well as other DCs. Reacting to these events, domestic import-competing industries have, paradoxically, started to demand and obtain protection from all import-competing sources including other DCs in the form of anti-dumping actions.[17]

It is also possible that the upsurge in intra-DC anti-dumping actions is linked to the fact that the DCs hardly file anti-dumping complaints before the GATT/WTO panels. As at the end of the Uruguay Round out of the seven anti-dumping cases heard by the GATT panels, the DCs had filed only one case.[18] Since then, even the transformation of the WTO dispute settlement system towards a stronger rules-based regime,[19] has not prompted them to challenge anti-dumping actions in particular. As at writing, the DCs have been complainants in only 36 of the reported anti-dumping cases. Moreover, 20 of these complaints have been initiated by only three DCs—

---

17. Whalley, John (1991). "Recent Trade Liberalization in the Developing World: What is Behind it and where is it Headed?" in David Greenaway, Robert C. Hine, Anthony P. O'Brien and Robert J. Thornton (eds.), *Global Protectionism*, London, Macmillan, p.225, pp.234-236; and Rajapatirana, Sarath and J. Luis Guash (1998). "Total Strangers or Soul Mates?—Anti-dumping and Competition Policies in Latin America and the Caribbean", *World Bank Policy Research Working Paper No.1958*, The World Bank, Washington DC, p.6.

18. Korea – Anti-Dumping Duties on Imports of Polyacetal Resins from the United States, Basic Instruments and Selected Documents of the GATT 40th Supplement, (1994), p. 205.

19. Montana, I Mora Miguel (1993). "A GATT with Teeth: Law Wins over Politics in International Trade Disputes", *Columbia Journal of Transnational Law*, 31, No. 1, p. 103.

Brazil (7 complaints[20]); India (5 complaints[21]); and Mexico (10 complaints[22]).

This general reluctance to argue cases is compounded further by the low-level of intra-DC anti-dumping cases. As at writing, the DCs that are the main targets of anti-dumping measures by other DCs hardly filed any complaints against these measures. PR China is yet to file any complaints; Chinese Taipei has filed one complaint against a measure by another DC;[23] the Republic of Korea has filed one complaint;[24] Brazil has filed 3 complaints;[25] India has filed 2 complaints;[26] and Indonesia has filed one complaint.[27] The DC that has been active in intra-DC complaints, relative to actions brought by other DCs is Mexico which has filed 5 complaints.[28] Such an attitude, has probably given off the signal that DCs are still prepared to acquiesce in anti-dumping cases and accept whatever action is taken against them, irrespective of whether their rights under the WTO Anti-dumping Agreement have been violated.

---

20. Argentina–Definitive Anti-Dumping Duties on Poultry from Brazil/DS241; EC – Customs Classification of Frozen Bone Chicken Cuts/DS269; EC – Anti-dumping Duties on Malleable Cast Iron Tube or Pipe Fittings/DS219; Mexico – Provisional Anti-Dumping Duties on Electrical Transformers/DS216; Turkey – Anti-Dumping Duty on Steel and Iron Pipe Fittings/DS208; US – Offset Act (Byrd Amendment)/DS217 (with Australia, Chile, European Communities, India, Indonesia, Japan, Korea and Thailand); and United States – Anti-dumping Duties on Silicon Metal from Brazil/DS239.
21. Brazil–Anti-Dumping Duties on Jute Bags from India/DS229; EC – Bed Linen/DS141; EC – Anti-Dumping Duties on Certain Flat Rolled Iron or Non-Alloy Steel Products from India/DS313; EC – Anti-Dumping Investigations Regarding Unbleached Cotton Fabrics from India/DS140; South Africa – Anti-Dumping Duties on Certain Pharmaceutical Products from India/DS168; and US – Anti-Dumping and Countervailing Measures on Steel Plate from India/DS206.
22. Ecuador–Definitive Anti-Dumping Measure on Cement from Mexico/DS191; Ecuador – Provisional Anti-Dumping Duties on Cement from Mexico/DS182; Guatemala – Cement I/DS60; Guatemala – Cement II/DS156; US – Anti-Dumping Measures on Cement/DS281; US – Anti-Dumping Measures on Oil Country Tubular Goods/DS282; US - Offset Act (Byrd Amendment, with Canada)/DS184; United States – Anti-Dumping Determinations Regarding Stainless Steel from Mexico/DS325; United States – Anti-Dumping Investigation Regarding Imports of Fresh Chilled Tomatoes from Mexico/DS49 and Venezuela – Anti-Dumping Investigation in Respect of Imports of Certain Oil Country Tubular Goods (OCTG)/DS23.
23. India–Anti-Dumping Measures on Certain Products from the Separate Customs Territory of Taiwan, Penghu, Kinmen and Matsu/DS318.
24. Philippines–Anti-Dumping Measures Regarding Polypropylene Resins from Korea/DS215.
25. See DS 208, DS 216 and DS 241, *supra*.
26. See DS 229 and DS168, *supra*.
27. Korea–Anti-Dumping Duties on Imports of Certain Paper from Indonesia/DS312.
28. See DS191, DS182, DS60, DS156, and DS23 *supra*.

The general impoverishment of DCs is also a factor to be considered in explaining their increasing reliance on anti-dumping actions. The point made in this regard is that there is a link between the ability of the state to fund social insurance programmes and its support for free trade. When national authorities can compensate those domestic interests that are seriously affected by trade liberalisation, they are less likely to obstruct progress towards an open trade regime.[29] In effect, the DCs' inclination towards protectionism stems in part from their general inability to fund domestic internal programmes of transfer payments that tend to arise in the wake of trade liberalisation.[30]

The role of domestic bureaucracies should be also examined when analysing the growing tendency by DCs to resort to anti-dumping actions. The general view of bureaucrats as public-spirited officials acting to serve the cause of the greater good is challenged by public choice theorists.[31] Public choice theory posits, *inter alia*, that public servants are motivated by, among other factors, institutional self-preservation.[32] Therefore, bureaucrats tend to exploit any range of opportunities to justify their existence. Anti-dumping actions provide such an opportunity. For instance, the government department involved in deciding whether to impose an anti-dumping duty on imports will invariably be required to ascertain whether dumping has occurred,[33] if the dumping has caused injury,[34] the anti-dumping duty to be imposed[35] or the price undertaking to be given.[36] Also, an anti-

29. Bates, Robert H.; Philip Brock and Jill Tiefenthaler (1991). "Risk and Trade Regimes: Another Exploration", 45, *International Organization*, No. 1, p. 1.

30. *ibid.*

31. An introduction to public choice theory is provided by James M. Buchanan (1984). "Politics without Romance: A Sketch of Positive Public Choice Theory and Its Normative Implications", in James M. Buchanan and Robert Tollison (eds.), *The Theory of Public Choice-II*, University of Michigan Press, Ann Arbor, p. 11.

32. *ibid.* p. 19; and Patrick Dunleavy (1991). *Democracy, Bureaucracy and Public Choice: Economic Explanations in Political Science*, Harvester Wheatsheaf. Hemel Hempstead, Hertfordshire, p.148 and pp.154-56. Public choice theory has been applied to international relations. Vaubel, Roland (1991). "A Public Choice View of International Organization", in Vaubel, Roland and Thomas D. Willett (eds.), *The Political Economy of International Organizations: a Public Choice Approach*, Westview Press, Boulder, Colorado, p. 27.

33. Agreement on Implementation of Article VI of the General Agreement on Tariffs and Trade 1994, available at *http://www.wto.org/English/docs_e/legal_e/19-adp-pdf*, Article 2.

34. *ibid.*, Article 3.

35. *ibid.*, Article 9.

36. *ibid.*, Article 8.

dumping action will involve additional administrative responsibilities such as reviewing petitions from commercial interests that feel threatened by foreign imports[37] and reviewing evidence submitted pursuant to an anti-dumping action.[38] In effect a number of bureaucratic procedures are needed to ascertain whether anti-dumping duties should be imposed or not. In addition, anti-dumping duties collected as a consequence of a finding of dumping and injury also add to the government revenues, revenues that provide for the sustenance of national bureaucracies.[39] Ever since the DCs' economic crisis of the 1980s, their bureaucrats have come under siege, their job prospects threatened by a raft of political and economic reforms.[40] Furthermore, revenue obtained from tariffs on imported goods is also under threat, if not already on the decline, as DCs cut their tariffs either unilaterally, or as a consequence of their membership of organisations such as the WTO.[41] Thus, anti-dumping duties are a good substitute for their lost income. Given the lack of response to anti-dumping actions at the WTO level, this income is best derived by targeting other DCs.

The Importance of Containing the Growing Problem of Intra-DC Anti-Dumping Actions

There are gains associated with trade liberalisation as it is a key ingredient of a constructive development strategy. This applies especially to the DCs. However, the DCs could abandon their current embrace of trade liberalisation. This could happen if they conclude that the world trading system works to impede their economic

37. *ibid.*, Article 5.

38. *ibid.*, Article 6.

39. Perhaps this explains the very high level of anti-dumping duties. On average, anti-dumping duties are 10 to 20 times higher than the MFN level, and it is not unheard of to have anti-dumping duties more than 100 times higher than the MFN level. See Prusa, *On the Spread and Impact of Anti-dumping, supra*, p. 4.

40. Jonah, Kwesi (1989). "The Social Impact of Ghana's Adjustment Programme, 1983-86", in *The IMF, the World Bank and the African Debt*, Vol. 2: *The Social and Political Impact*, Bade Onimode (ed.), Zed Books: London, p. 149, pp. 141-44; and Richard, L. Harris and Melinda J. Seid (2000). "Critical Perspectives on Globalization and Neoliberalism in the Developing Countries", XVI *Journal of Developing Societies*, No.1, p. 1, pp. 12-13.

41. Whether the DCs have the administrative capabilities to undertake a thorough anti-dumping investigation and arrive at an accurate determination as to whether there has been dumping and injury is a moot point. Krueger, Anne O. (1995). *Trade Policies and Developing Nations*, The Brookings Institution, Washington DC, pp. 64-65.

development.[42] The received wisdom is that DC exports encounter serious barriers in developed country markets. One solution to this has always been the argument that South-South trade can serve as an outlet for goods from the DCs. Thus if intra-DC trade is stifled, then there will continue to be a threat to the multilateral trading system. Hence it is vital for the development strategies of the South that South-South trade be encouraged and developed further. What worsens this is that intra-DC anti-dumping actions will most probably increase given the edge that this tool of protection has over the safeguard provisions in the agreement on agriculture.[43] During the Uruguay Round, the members of the WTO agreed to draft rules to govern world trade in agriculture. To prevent domestic markets from dislocation on account of the increased trade the agreement on agriculture contains special safeguards provisions and these can be invoked in certain circumstances.[44]

However, the operation of this special safeguard clause is to be carried out in a transparent manner with the applicant member being bound by procedural requirements that include giving the Committee on Agriculture (CAG)[45] advance notice of such action,[46] affording any members affected by its action the opportunity to consult with it in respect of the conditions of application of such action[47] and supplying data to the CAG with regard to the safeguard action taken.[48] In effect, definite import levels are to be reached and procedural guidelines adhered to, before trade-restricting measures can be adopted under the agreement on agriculture.

Under the anti-dumping agreement, however, there is no provision for supranational consultation prior to the initiation of an investigation and the imposition of an anti-dumping duty. All that is required is a petition from a domestic industry to the national anti-dumping authority.[49] Thus, it is this that import-competing interests

---

42. Stiglitz, Joseph (1999). "Trade and the Developing World: A New Agenda", 99 *Current History*, No. 631 p. 387, p. 339.

43. Agreement on Agriculture, available at *http://www.wto.org/English/docs_e/legal_e-ag.pdf.*

44. *ibid.*, Article 5 (1).

45. The Committee on Agriculture is established under Article 17, *ibid.*

46. Article 7, *ibid.*

47. *ibid.*

48. *ibid.*

49. See Anti-dumping Agreement, *supra*, Article 5 (1).

can easily exploit. The role played by the Committee on Anti-Dumping Practices (CADP) is not as robust as the role of the CAG. The only obligation on the members is to report all preliminary or final anti-dumping determinations to the CADP.[50] The import of this is that with an increase in trade in agricultural goods, there is likely to be an increase in anti-dumping actions but this will probably not be under the agreement on agriculture. Agricultural products are the main exports of the developing countries and thus anti-dumping actions in this respect will lessen any benefits they can derive from the multilateral trading system and so weaken their confidence in the same.

Possible Measures to Combat LDC Tendencies for Anti-Dumping Actions

In light of the above analysis it is obvious that tighter control over domestic anti-dumping investigating authorities in DCs is needed. This can be done through a reform of the Anti-dumping Agreement as well as through measures adopted by DCs at the national and regional level. The remaining part of this chapter suggests some options to be explored in this regard.

One recent development in some DCs is the creation of new trade policy-making institutions that reflect the national interest instead of parochial interests.[51] In certain instances these institutions have assumed responsibility for anti-dumping actions. For example, Brazil has made trade policy making more responsive to national interests by creating a more neutral institution. Columbia has also brought trade policy making under the aegis of the Ministry of Foreign Trade and established stringent criteria for anti-dumping actions.[52] In the view of some observers these institutions follow transparent processes which, compared to the past are a marked improvement.[53] Venezuela's anti-dumping regime is also administered by a specialised independent agency[54] that is supposed to act as an impartial arbiter between domestic producers and importers.[55] Thus, the creation of new,

50. *ibid.*, Article 16 (4).
51. See Guash and Rajapatirana, "Total Strangers or Soul Mates?" *supra*, p. 14.
52. *ibid.*
53. *ibid.*, p. 15.
54. Castro-Bernieri, Jorge and Paul Anthony Levine (1996). "The Venezuelan Anti-dumping and Countervailing Duties Regime", *Journal of World Trade*, 30, No. 1, pp. 125-126.
55. *ibid.*, pp. 127–28.

accountable, and transparent trade institutions by DCs, or the strengthening of existing ones to administer and/or monitor anti-dumping investigations is necessary, as they can serve to restrain arbitrary action designed to appease well-organised domestic import-competing lobbies.

Generally, anti-dumping actions are bad for trade liberalisation. However, the political reality is that more and more countries are inclined to use anti-dumping actions to protect their markets. As a consequence, the DCs should also insist on a provision in any revised agreement that obliges all WTO members to enact anti-dumping legislation by a given date. The current position in the anti-dumping agreement is that it only imposes an obligation on the members to ensure that their anti-dumping laws and regulations are consistent with the provisions of the anti-dumping agreement[56] and, to also notify the CADP of any changes in their anti-dumping laws and regulations.[57] In effect, there is no need for legislation: administrative practices can suffice. This, I argue, enables covert anti-dumping activity that is not subject to the rules in the anti-dumping agreement.[58]

As at writing, some DC WTO Members rely on administrative discretion to shelter domestic industries from foreign competition pleading, as usual, that they do not have the expertise or know-how to draft anti-dumping legislation. This plea, as I have argued elsewhere, is a misrepresentation of the facts and, rather, DCs have largely been conversant with anti-dumping laws.[59] Moreover, it is hard to accept this alibi given that so many DCs have enacted complex economic legislation such as investment and company codes. Thus, I believe that it is possible for DCs to enact anti-dumping legislation provided there is the political desire (and pressure) to do so. In addition, demanding that all WTO members enact anti-dumping legislation can promote certainty in anti-dumping investigations and thus restrain the abuse of opaque administrative discretionary power

56. See Anti-dumping Agreement, *supra*, Article 18 (4).

57. *ibid.*, Article 18 (5).

58. Kufuor, Kofi Oteng (2004). "The Development of Anti-dumping Policy and Practice in Ghana from Independence to the Present", University of East London International Trade *Forum Discussion Paper*, available at *http://www.uel.ac.uk/law/research/publications/index.htm*.

59. See Kufour, "Developing Countries and the Shaping of GATT/WTO Anti-dumping Law", *supra*, pp. 172–73.

by bureaucrats and their domestic protectionist allies. As a consequence, component parts of the global trading regime will move their trade policy from a power-oriented approach towards a rules-oriented approach.[60] Such a development can only further enhance the rule of law in the world trading system as a whole.

The DCs could also rely on regional organisations to provide a code to govern all members of the organisation who are yet to draft anti-dumping legislation.[61] Moreover, DC regional organisations could assume responsibility for monitoring intra-DC anti-dumping actions.[62] Trade sectors where dumping and injury are repeatedly alleged could be closely examined by these organisations with comments made as to whether there is a genuine need for protection through anti-dumping actions. This would probably increase pressure on protectionist forces by making them aware of the fact that they are known to stifle regional and global trade. Such information can help identify hostile as well as friendly DC markets and thus allow for exporters to have some predictability in their business decisions.

In addition to this monitoring role, DC regional integration organisations could assist DC exporters with the procedural and technical requirements to be met when responding to anti-dumping investigations if such assistance is ever required. Regional integration organisations could also make certain that actions being taken by petitioners are consistent with the WTO Anti-dumping Agreement. Furthermore, information gathered by regional organisations can help

60. The importance of a rules-based multilateral trading system is discussed in Jackson, John H. (1978). "The Crumbling Institutions of the Liberal Trade System", 12 *Journal of World Trade Law* No. 1, pp. 93-98; and "Statement of GATT Director–General Arthur Dunkel", reprinted in part in, *Legal Problems of International Economic Relations*, (1995) (3rd. ed.) John H. Jackson, William J. Davey and Alan O. Sykes jr., (eds.), West Publishing Co., St. Paul Minnesota, p. 251.

61. For instance, Mercosur's members have signed an agreement on the application of anti-dumping measures against imports from third countries. Although this agreement does not create common rules for Mercosur's members it constitutes a legal framework with which national regulations must comply. This agreement thus forms the foundation of the future Mercosur Anti-dumping Code. Barral, Welber and Gilvan Brogini, *Anti-dumping in Mercosur*, available at *http://www.wtexec.com/Ib033199.html*.

62. Some regional organisations with a large DC membership are already playing a role in anti-dumping issues. For instance, the Organization of American States has 35 members, all of which except Canada and the United States are DCs. The OAS and the Inter-American System, pp.6-7, available at *http://www.oas.org/en/pINFO/OAS/oas.htm*. In 1995 it established Working Groups to recommend action on, *inter alia* anti-dumping measures. Permanent Council of the Organization of American States Special Committee on Inter–American Summits Management, available at *http://www.summit-americas.org/CEGCI%20DOCS/CE-GCI-12-95-rev-1-eng-html*.

restrain the increasing DC tendency to attack other DCs with anti-dumping investigations.

One issue that was not fully resolved in the Uruguay Round was that of the public interest in anti-dumping actions. In its current form the Anti-dumping Agreement just requires that notice of an investigation be given to petitioners and respondents (and other interested parties).[63] At present, therefore, the consideration of import-competing producer interests dominates the rationale for anti-dumping laws. However, there is nothing to indicate that there is an interface between the objectives of import-competing interests and the interests of wider society. Thus, a public interest clause in a revised anti-dumping agreement could serve as a means of access to socio-economic justice for DC citizens. However, it should be noted here that citizen activism in DCs is not as robust as it is in the developed countries. Years of authoritarian rule have stifled the emergence and development of a strong civil society capable of championing citizen's rights. Although the situation is changing and NGOs are beginning to share the political space that was once the monopoly of the state, it is not unreasonable to assume that a very strong civil society is still a fairly distant prospect. This lack of a dynamic activist base can thus thwart any attempts to advance the public interest in anti-dumping actions. Building up the capacity of civil society will therefore be of critical importance.

Action at the national and regional level should support litigation by DCs before the WTO. As I have noted elsewhere, the DCs must litigate to defend their rights in the WTO system.[64] Repeat litigation has its advantages.[65] Some scholars have even argued that merely initiating a dispute under the WTO Dispute Settlement Understanding can induce changes in behaviour that is allegedly inconsistent with any of the WTO's Agreements.[66] Hence to secure greater openness of the world trading system and to protect their

---

63. See Anti-dumping Agreement, *supra*, Article 12 (1).
64. Kufour, Kofi Oteng (1997). "From the GATT to the WTO: The Developing Countries and the Reform of the Procedures for the Settlement of International Trade Dispute", *Journal of World Trade*, 31, No. 5, p. 117, p.141.
65. Galanter, Marc (1974). "Why the "Haves" Come out Ahead: Speculations on the Limits of Legal Change", *Law and Society Review*, 9, No. 1, p. 95.
66. Steger, Debra P. and Susan M. Hainsworth (1998). "World Trade Organization Dispute Settlement: The First Three Years", *Journal of International Economic Law*, 1, No. 2, p. 199, p. 204.

rights under the WTO, the DCs should file complaints before the WTO panels alleging breaches of the Anti-dumping Agreement whenever they deem this appropriate.

Another measure to prevent intra-DC anti-dumping conflicts is that the class of persons defined by the Anti-dumping Agreement as interested partiers with rights to defend their interests in anti-dumping hearings,[67] to present oral evidence,[68] receive oral information given during hearing,[69] and see all non-confidential information relevant to their cases,[70] should be expanded to include representatives of consumer organisations. Under current rules of evidence in the Agreement representatives of consumer organisations can be defined as "interested parties" only if members conducting an investigation extend this privilege to them. In addition the investigating authorities are only to allow representatives of consumer organisations to provide information in cases where the product under investigation is "commonly sold at the retail level".[71] The aim of this provision is to enable consumer organisations provide any information that is relevant to an investigation. However, the problem here is that considerable discretion will be needed to ascertain what amounts to information relevant to an investigation. Besides, there is no obligation on the national investigating authority to act in accordance with the information so supplied. My contention therefore, is that as long as consumer organisations have no rights but merely privileges, investigating authorities conducting an anti-dumping action are hardly likely to take their views seriously. Therefore, widening access to anti-dumping investigations, so as to allow consumer organisations to influence decision-making will most probably serve to restrain national authorities from disregarding citizen's interest.

As we noted above, the inability of DC governments to provide social insurance for domestic interests harmed by low-priced imports is one of the factors that explain the increasing tendency towards anti-dumping actions. A possible solution to this is that DC policy-makers compensate domestic interests. On the face of it, this suggestion smacks of state intervention and is therefore *prima facie* contrary to the

67. See Anti-dumping Agreement, *supra*, Article 6 (2).

68. *ibid.*

69. *ibid.*, Article 6 (3).

70. *ibid.*, Article 6 (11).

71. *ibid.*, Article 6 (12).

principles of free trade. Nevertheless, the proposal has its merits that at least warrant further discussion.

First, one major threat to the WTO system as a whole is its political feasibility. Social movements and some of the WTO's very members are beginning to question the legitimacy of the global trading system as it stands.[72] Thus, compensation to interests affected as a consequence of dumped goods serves to make free trade more acceptable. Second, trade barriers are a hidden source of taxation to consumers, costing them billions of dollars each year and begetting myriad other inefficiencies in their wake. The ideal solution then is for consumers to compensate the losers for their losses and thus accomplish the end goal of free trade. In effect some portion of the wealth generated by comparative advantage must be redirected to interests that have suffered as a consequence of trade liberalisation.[73] Ideally this should be done through, consumers directly compensating free trade's losers.

The problem here though is that transaction costs are an obstacle to such a deal because most individual consumers do not have money at stake either to organise or to participate in such an action.[74] The solution therefore is for the state to complete the transaction that the parties subject to protection would strike among themselves if transaction costs were not prohibitive.[75] But given budgetary constraints in the DCs, multilateral development institutions committed to trade liberalisation should either support national initiatives or assume full responsibility for this proposed wealth transfer.

Either way, DC consumer interests will be protected through access to low-priced goods or, negatively affected sectors of DC societies will be compensated for losses incurred. Thus the free trade orthodoxy championed by institutions such as the World Bank will become more acceptable to countries and interests that are still

---

72. Gill, Stephen (2000). "Towards a Postmodern Prince? The Battle in Seattle as Movement in the New Politics of Globalization", Millennium: *Journal of International Studies*, 29, No. 1, pp. 131-40.

73. Chen, Jim (2000). "Globalization and its Losers", Minnesota *Journal of Global Trade*, 9, No. 1, p. 157, p. 212.

74. Dudley, David (1998). "The Coase Theorem as Applied to Trade barriers and Optimal Adjustment Strategies", University of Pennsylvania *Journal of International Economic Law*, 19, No. 4, p. 1029, p. 1031.

75. *ibid.*

somewhat sceptical of the idea. However, it is also extremely important to note that wholesale compensation to displaced industries will be self-defeating. It would probably kill off competition, as firms would not need to innovate and discipline costs to survive since there would always be the promise of handouts to shield them from foreign competition. Therefore, there should be transparent preconditions before compensation can be paid out. A useful guide can be Article 3 of the Anti-Dumping Agreement. These provisions state that injury is caused only if domestic competition interests are not harmed as a result of a range of factors.[76] Applying the same to compensation for losers could serve as notice that protection from dumped goods should not be taken for granted.

76. The Anti-dumping Agreement states that an examination of the impact of dumped goods on the importing industry should take into account all other relevant factors and indices that have a bearing on the state of the industry. See Anti-dumping Agreement, *supra*, Article 3 (4).

5

The Rhetoric and Reality of US Anti-Dumping Law

BRINK LINDSEY and DANIEL IKENSON[1]

Introduction

Anti-dumping laws allow national governments to impose special duties on 'unfairly traded' imports. Before duties are imposed, the authorities that administer the law must make two findings: (1) that imported goods are being 'dumped', or sold at prices less than 'normal value', and (2) that the dumped imports are causing or threatening material injury to the domestic import-competing industry. Under the US system, the Department of Commerce (DOC) determines whether dumping is occurring, while the International Trade Commission (ITC) examines whether dumped imports are causing injury to the domestic industry. When both the DOC and the ITC make affirmative findings, the goods under investigation are subject to duties equal to the margin of dumping—that is, the difference between the US prices of the imports and their 'normal value'.

Supporters of anti-dumping laws argue that they are needed to create a 'level playing field' for domestic industries that face unfair import competition. Specifically, they contend that various distortions in foreign markets—trade barriers, monopoly or collusion, government subsidies, and 'barriers to exit' (e.g., poor bankruptcy laws, ineffective protection of creditors' rights) that prevent loss-making businesses from reducing capacity or going out of business—allow foreign producers to charge lower prices in export markets than would otherwise be possible. In one scenario, firms may enjoy supernormal profits at home (in a protected or cartelised 'sanctuary market') and then use those profits to cross-subsidise low-price export sales. Alternatively, subsidies or barriers to exit may allow firms to sell

1. This chapter is excerpted from a book by the same authors entitled: *Anti-dumping Exposed: The Devilish Details of Unfair Trade Law*, Washington, DC, Cato Institute, 2003.

abroad (and at home as well) at below-cost prices without suffering the normal marketplace consequences.

According to supporters, anti-dumping laws ensure a level playing field by offsetting artificial sources of competitive advantage. Dumping, it is alleged, demonstrates the existence of one or more of the market distortions discussed above; anti-dumping duties, by making up the difference between dumped prices and 'normal value', extinguish the foreign producer's artificial advantage and put the domestic industry back on an equal footing. At least that is the theory.

There is, however, a yawning gap between theory and practice. Anti-dumping laws, contrary to the claims of their supporters, do not ensure a level playing field. Instead, they penalise foreign producers for engaging in commercial practices that are perfectly legal and unexceptionable when engaged in by domestic companies. Such discrimination against foreign firms creates an unlevel playing field for imports. In other words, anti-dumping laws discriminate against imports, and that is the essence of protectionism.

Unfortunately, this particular form of protectionism enjoys the sanction of multilateral trading rules. Article VI of the original General Agreement on Tariffs and Trade authorises national governments to impose duties on dumped imports. Today, the authority to engage in anti-dumping protectionism is recognised by the World Trade Organization. The WTO Anti-dumping Agreement, finalised in 1994 during the Uruguay Round of trade talks, specifies the standards and procedures that national anti-dumping regulations must follow. Although the requirements of this agreement do impose modest restraint on what WTO members can do in the name of anti-dumping, the sad fact is that the agreement allows wide scope for protectionist abuses.

In recent years, many countries have been urging the US government to agree to new international rules at the World Trade Organization that would tighten the requirements that must be met before anti-dumping protection can be granted. But powerful US lobbying interests, and their supporters in Congress, have vehemently opposed such changes in anti-dumping rules. American industries that frequently seek anti-dumping protection argue that a 'strong' law is needed to ensure a level playing field and to maintain public support for generally open markets. They insist that any effort to 'weaken' current law through trade negotiations must be rejected out of hand. Unfortunately, there is broad political support for this perspective from Republicans and Democrats alike.

What accounts for this enduring, bipartisan popularity? In the first place, the law's rhetoric is compelling. After all, which members of Congress would like to stand up and say they favour illegal and unfair dumped imports? Who could be opposed to a level playing field? Meanwhile, the reality behind the rhetoric is obscure. The anti-dumping law is notoriously complicated, and its inner workings are known only to a select handful of users, targets, bureaucrats, and lawyers. As a result, most supporters of the law simply take its appealing rhetoric at face value. If it sounds good, it must be good.

Advocates of the US anti-dumping law claim that dumping is an unfair trade practice that takes two different forms: price discrimination and below-cost sales. Both types of dumping allegedly reflect underlying market distortions caused by foreign government policies. Those distortions confer an artificial advantage on foreign producers when they are selling in the United States—they can sell at lower prices than would otherwise be possible.

Thus, price discrimination (i.e., selling at lower prices in the export market than at home) supposedly signals the existence of a protected 'sanctuary' home market. According to Greg Mastel, one of the few economists who firmly support the use of anti-dumping laws:

> If a company engages in dumping in foreign markets and its home market is open, the price differential will induce the company's competitors or other resellers to re-export dumped products to the dumper's home market. These re-exports would quickly pull the home market price down to the dumped price and erase home market profits. Thus, a closed or restricted home market is also a virtual precondition to a successful dumping strategy.[2]

This situation gives the foreign producer an arguably unfair competitive advantage over US rivals. "A closed home market allows companies to charge high prices at home because they face no foreign competition," Mastel explains. "Foreign companies can then use the profits from these domestic sales to cross-subsidise export sales at dumped prices."[3]

---

2. Mastel, Greg (1998). *Anti-dumping Laws and the US Economy,* Armonk, N.Y: M. E. Sharpe, p. 43.

3. *ibid.*, p. 41.

As to sales below cost, the contention is that the foreign producer could not sustain its losses in the absence of market-distorting government policies back home. Here again, a domestic sanctuary market could be the culprit: profits at home could allow a company to take losses abroad. Alternatively, government subsidies could prop up a company in spite of its losses. The subsidies might take the form of explicit grants or soft loans, or they might be considerably subtler.

But does anti-dumping practice match its rhetoric? Are anti-dumping duties, for better or worse, really offsetting the effects of market-distorting government policies? These questions need to be answered in two stages. First, it is necessary to determine the effectiveness of current anti-dumping methodologies at targeting the supposedly unfair pricing practices of price discrimination and selling below cost. Second, to the extent that the anti-dumping law does indeed find its targets, it must be ascertained whether those pricing practices are reliable indicators of underlying market distortions.

Missing the Target

The first step in this inquiry is to review in broad brush how dumping is actually calculated under US law. In general, the DOC compares the prices of imported merchandise sold in the United States to some measure of 'normal value'. There are, however, a number of different ways to perform such comparisons—and in particular, a number of different benchmarks for determining normal value.

In the most familiar method, the DOC compares 'net' US prices to 'net' home-market prices. To arrive at net values, the DOC subtracts freight charges, brokerage and handling fees, commissions, and various other selling expenses; the idea here is to compare prices on an 'ex factory' basis.

The anti-dumping statute indicates that comparing US and home-market prices is the preferred method of calculating dumping margins. If specified conditions exist, though, the DOC will employ alternative methodologies. Thus, if the foreign producer does not sell the subject merchandise in the domestic market, or its total domestic sales are less than five per cent of its US sales, the home market is considered not viable. In that case the DOC will select another export market to serve as the comparison market; US prices are then compared to prices in some third-country market. If there are no viable third-country markets, the DOC will compare US prices to 'constructed value'—which is equal to the company's total cost of production plus some amount for profit.

The DOC can deviate from normal price-to-price comparisons even when there is a viable domestic or third-country market. Within the broad category of merchandise under investigation, there may be many different specific product types or models. For each model sold in the United States, the DOC tries to identify sales of identical or similar products in the comparison market; if it cannot find any such sales, the US sales of that model will be compared to constructed value.

More important, the DOC examines comparison-market prices to determine whether they are below the full cost of production. If more than 20 per cent of comparison-market prices of a particular model are below cost, the DOC will exclude all the below-cost sales of that model from its calculations on the ground that they are "outside the ordinary course of trade". In that case, US prices are compared to above-cost comparison-market prices only; if there are no above-cost sales of identical or similar merchandise, US prices are compared to constructed value.

The DOC employs another methodology altogether for imports from 'non-market economies' (NMEs), that is, China, Vietnam, and a few members of the former Soviet bloc. In NME cases, DOC rejects prices as unreliable, since they are not the product of genuine market transactions. Constructed value is also rejected on the ground that the company's costs are likewise not market based. Instead, the DOC obtains the company's 'factors of production'—the physical quantities of all the inputs used in producing the merchandise—and values those inputs on the basis of prices in a 'surrogate country'. Surrogate countries are market economies judged to be at a level of economic development similar to that of the NME country in question. The DOC then compares US prices to a cost-based normal value derived from company-specific factors of production and surrogate-country prices of those factors (including surrogate-country averages for selling, general, and administrative expenses and profit).

Finally, the DOC sometimes calculates dumping on the basis of 'facts available' rather than actual company data. Determinations are based on facts available when a foreign producer fails to provide all the price and cost information requested by the DOC, or when the information provided is judged to be inaccurate or incomplete (an ever-present possibility given the byzantine complexity of documentation that foreign companies are required to provide). In those situations, the facts available used by the DOC are generally derived from the allegations contained in the domestic industry's anti-dumping petition.

What do the various calculation methodologies have to do with finding either price discrimination or sales below cost? As it turns out, not very much. As to price discrimination, only one methodology even attempts to measure relevant international price differences; and none of the methodologies seek to determine whether sales below cost are occurring.

Of all the different ways that the DOC measures dumping, only the straightforward comparison of home-market and US prices is capable of identifying price discrimination that reflects a protected sanctuary market. On the other hand, the apparent price discrimination may be nothing more than an artefact of imperfect price comparisons.

Flawed Methodologies

In the typical anti-dumping investigation, the DOC compares home-market and US prices of physically different goods, in different kinds of packaging, sold at different times, in different and fluctuating currencies, to different customers at different levels of trade, in different quantities, with different freight and other movement costs, different credit terms, and other differences in directly associated selling expenses (e.g., commissions, warranties, royalties, and advertising). Is it any wonder that the prices are not identical?

Admittedly, the DOC's dumping calculation methodologies try to adjust for some of the differences, but the adjustments are necessarily imprecise. For example, when the DOC compares physically different merchandise, it adjusts for differences in materials, direct labour, and variable overhead costs. While this makes a certain amount of sense, in a real-world commercial context it goes without saying that actual price differences may be more or less than the differences in variable manufacturing costs. And in many cases, the DOC makes no adjustment. Thus, prices of goods sold in the United States may be compared to prices of goods sold many months earlier or later in the home market without any adjustment for market fluctuations over the intervening time. And although unit prices typically decline with larger order quantities, the DOC rarely adjusts for quantity discounts.

Critics of anti-dumping have focused considerable attention on asymmetries in the DOC's methodologies that produce a bias in favour of finding price differences.[4] Without a doubt, such asymmetries exist. But the more fundamental and too often neglected problem is that the practice of comparing each and every US sale to some sale in the home market will produce spurious price differences that are purely the product of 'apples-and-oranges' comparisons.

Whatever be the problems associated with comparing home-market and US prices, at least such comparisons bear directly on the question of international price discrimination and possible sanctuary markets. By contrast, the other methodologies have nothing to do with finding relevant international price differences.

Thus, a comparison of US and third-country prices can possibly show international price discrimination, but it cannot reveal a sanctuary market. Any foreign producer under investigation is an 'outsider' as far as all third-country markets are concerned; it is hindered, not helped, by any government barriers that block access to its export sales. If for some reason the company is earning higher prices in that third country, the reason clearly is not that government-imposed barriers are shielding it from competition. On the contrary, it had to overcome any barriers that were present in that third-country market to be selling there at all. Meanwhile, prices charged in a third country indicate nothing about whether a firm's home market is closed.

Comparison of US prices to a cost-based normal value—whether it is derived from the company's own costs (in constructed-value cases) or from surrogate-country prices (in NME cases)—cannot show price discrimination, for the simple reason that price data are not used for one side of the comparison. Furthermore, a finding of dumping using constructed value offers no evidence of the existence of a sanctuary home market. All such a finding can show is that US sales are being made below some baseline level of profitability; it cannot show that home-market sales are above any similar baseline, since home-market sales are excluded from the dumping calculation.

4. Biases in anti-dumping methodologies are reviewed extensively in Brink Lindsey and Daniel Ikenson (2002). "Anti-dumping 101: The Devilish Details of 'Unfair Trade' Law", *Cato Trade Policy Analysis* No. 20, November 26.

Indeed, when constructed value is used because there are no above-cost sales of identical or similar merchandise in the home market, the available evidence weighs against the existence of a sanctuary market. A sanctuary market is one in which a foreign company is making profits due to government intervention; here, though, the company is apparently losing money at home. The supposed source of unfair advantage—namely, the opportunity to cross-subsidise low-price export sales—is missing.

The situation is similar when US sales are compared to above-cost sales only. A dumping finding based on such comparisons tells us nothing about the existence of international price discrimination, since the comparisons are skewed: low-price sales have been excluded from the home-market side, but not the US side. And here again, as in constructed-value cases, the evidence affirmatively rebuts claims of a sanctuary market. Below-cost sales are excluded only when they constitute at least 20 per cent of sales; such widespread losses are inconsistent with the supposedly supernormal profits of a sanctuary market.

Finally, a dumping finding based on facts available provides no evidence of either price discrimination or a sanctuary market. The facts available are generally taken from the domestic industry's anti-dumping petition, hardly a source of objective analysis. Indeed, it is expressly recognised that determinations on the basis of facts available are punitive; it is the threat of such determinations that is used to compel foreign producers' cooperation with the DOC's often onerous information requests.[5] In any event, the dumping allegations in anti-dumping petitions are often based on estimates of constructed value, and thus are incapable of substantiating the existence of price discrimination or a sanctuary market.

If the anti-dumping law takes poor aim at price discrimination, it fires completely blindly when it comes to sales below cost. Not one of the methodologies employed by the DOC measures whether imported merchandise is sold at a loss. The DOC does determine whether home-market or third-country sales are below cost in deciding whether to exclude them as "outside the ordinary course of

---

5. The anti-dumping statute authorises the DOC, in making a "facts available" determination because a foreign producer has failed to cooperate, to "use an inference that is adverse to the interests of that party". Section 776(b) of the Tariff Act of 1930, as amended, codified at 19 U.S.C. § 1677e(b).

trade". That inquiry, though, is irrelevant to the issue of whether US sales are below cost.

The closest the DOC comes to determining whether US sales are made at a loss is in constructed-value and NME cases. In those cases, the DOC does calculate the production costs of the merchandise sold in the United States,[6] but then it adds an amount for profit before the resulting normal value is compared to US sales prices. Thus, the criterion for deciding whether imports are unfairly traded under this methodology is, not the existence of losses, but insufficient profitability. Sales at a loss are considered dumped, but so are profitable sales if the profit rate is too low.

That over-inclusiveness is exacerbated by the specific way in which dumping margins are calculated in cost-based cases. The DOC compares average US prices of specific models to a single product-wide or industry-wide profitability rate. Sales below the profitability benchmark are considered dumped; sales above the benchmark are deemed to have dumping margins of zero. Consequently, even if US sales average a 'normal' profit, dumping will be found simply because profit rates vary by model.

Finally, there is an additional layer of methodological distortion in NME cases. In those cases, the cost data used are not those of the firm under investigation; instead, surrogate values from another country are applied to that firm's factors of production. This methodology is fraught with potential for gross inaccuracy. The extent to which the end result bears any relation to market-based costs is open to serious question.

Examining the Case Record

To evaluate the problems with current anti-dumping practice in fuller detail, we examined all DOC final determinations through December 31, 1998, in original anti-dumping investigations initiated since January 1, 1995. This sample includes 141 company-specific dumping determinations in 49 different anti-dumping investigations.[7]

6. In constructed-value cases the costs used are the foreign producer's own, whereas in NME cases costs are calculated by valuing the foreign producer's 'factors of production' according to price data from a surrogate market-economy country.

7. DOC investigations are specific to a particular product from a particular country. In a single investigation, though, the DOC may calculate separate dumping margins for numerous different foreign producers.

The DOC made affirmative dumping findings for 107 of the 141 companies investigated and in 48 of the 49 investigations. The average dumping margin in the sample, including all the zero and *de minimis* dumping findings,[8] is 44.68 per cent.

The most striking fact that emerges from a review of these case records is how few anti-dumping determinations have anything to do with targeting—or even attempting to target—price discrimination associated with possible sanctuary markets. Price discrimination bulks very large in anti-dumping rhetoric but commands much less attention in actual anti-dumping practice.

Of the 141 total determinations, 36 were based on facts available rather than actual company data.[9] Another 47 of the determinations are from the 14 NME investigations included in the sample. In 16 of the determinations, constructed value was used either because there was no viable comparison market or because there were no identical or similar products sold in the comparison market. For 37 determinations, at least 20 per cent of the sales of some or all comparison products were below cost, so the DOC compared US prices to some combination of comparison-market prices, above-cost comparison-market prices only, and constructed value. And one determination was based purely on a comparison of US and third-country prices.

That leaves only 4 determinations in which the DOC calculated dumping strictly on the basis of comparisons of US and home-market prices. Furthermore, in 2 of the 4 determinations in question, the DOC concluded that there was zero or *de minimis* dumping. Thus, in only 2 of the 107 total affirmative determinations (both of which were made in the same investigation) did the DOC find dumping by relying exclusively on the currently used calculation methodology that bears any possible connection to the existence of market-distorted price discrimination.

Another 31 determinations, encompassing 17 different investigations, relied partially on comparisons of US and home-market

8. In original anti-dumping investigations, any dumping margin of less than two per cent is considered *de minimis* and effectively equal to zero.

9. For 34 of the 36 determinations, the DOC relied entirely on 'facts available'; in other words, it made no use whatsoever of information provided by the foreign producers. For two of the determinations the DOC relied on a combination of foreign producers' information and facts available. These two determinations were included because in both cases the partial use of facts available was both extensive and punitive (i.e. the DOC purposefully selected adverse facts).

prices.[10] In all of those determinations, however, the DOC skewed at least some of the comparisons by using only above-cost home-market sales, or by substituting constructed value for actual price data. In those mixed cases, the DOC found dumping in 25 of the determinations. For those determinations, however, it is impossible to tell from the public record how much of each dumping margin is attributable to normal comparisons of US and home-market prices, how much to comparisons of US prices and above-cost prices only, and how much to comparisons of US prices and constructed value. In other words, there is insufficient publicly available information to distinguish between the 'signal' of international price differences and the 'noise' of dumping margins generated by methodologies that do not detect price differences.

There are good grounds for assuming that the 'noise' is considerable. Mixing methodologies tends to increase dumping margins above what would be found if only normal price-to-price comparisons were made. Comparing US sales to only above-cost sales always exaggerates dumping margins, since all the lowest-price sales are excluded from the comparison. And resort to constructed value often exaggerates dumping margins because of the artificially high profit rates that are frequently used.[11]

In sum, a review of the actual case record confirms that the anti-dumping law as currently written and implemented is miserably ineffective at identifying price discrimination caused by sanctuary markets. In only 27 of the 107 affirmative determinations, or 25.2 per cent of that total, did the DOC make at least some use of the only methodology relevant to detecting price discrimination, and all but 2 of those determinations were distorted by resort to other methodologies. Meanwhile, in the other 80 affirmative determinations, or 74.8 per cent of the total, there is absolutely nothing in the DOC's findings that in any way points to the existence of price discrimination.

What about the anti-dumping law's track record with respect to the other form of dumping—below-cost sales caused by market

10. This figure is a subset of the 37 determinations mentioned above in which the DOC partially or totally rejected home-market or third-country comparison product sales. This smaller figure excludes those determinations in which any third-country sales were used and those in which all comparison-market sales were rejected.

11. See 'Anti-dumping 101' for a more in-depth treatment of this issue.

distortions? In as many as 100 of the 141 determinations in the sample, the DOC relied fully or partially on cost-based analysis. Nearly half of the determinations—67 of 141—depend exclusively on comparisons of US prices to some cost-based benchmark of normal value. In 20 of those cases, the DOC used the foreign producer's own cost information to calculate constructed value;[12] the remaining 47 were NME cases in which the DOC calculated costs using surrogate-country values. In an additional 33 determinations, the DOC made at least some use of constructed value in its calculations, although perhaps not in every determination.[13]

The most obvious problem with all of the cost-based determinations is that they do not attempt to measure whether US sales are below cost. As discussed above, they measure instead whether US sales are below some measure of cost plus profit. Because of the inclusion of profit, sales can be considered dumped even when they are above cost, and the dumping margins of below-cost sales are exaggerated.

Market Distortions Assumed, Not Proven

The evidence reviewed shows that the anti-dumping law is highly prone to finding dumping even when there is no price discrimination or selling below cost. But there is another deeper problem with the law. Namely, it simply assumes that those pricing practices, when found, indicate the existence of government-caused market distortions. As shown below, this assumption is entirely unwarranted.

It is true that international price differences can reveal a sanctuary home market. Likewise, sales below cost, under certain circumstances, can signal the presence of government-caused market distortions. But just the fact that they can does not mean that they usually do. There

12. This total consists of 16 determinations in which the DOC used constructed value because of an absence of viable comparison markets or similar comparison products, and another 4 determinations in which publicly available information makes clear that the DOC rejected all comparison-market sales as below cost and therefore relied exclusively on constructed value.

13. The total consists of the 31 'mixed' cases discussed above, plus an additional 2 determinations in which the DOC rejected at least some third-country sales as below cost and instead relied either on above-cost third-country sales or constructed value. In those 33 determinations, it cannot be determined with certainty from the public record whether the DOC in fact used constructed value in every instance (such use would be unnecessary if there were any above-cost sales of the comparison products), nor can the extent to which constructed value was used be determined.

are many other possible explanations—explanations that rest entirely on normal business practices and have nothing to do with any 'unfair' competitive advantage. By assuming that margins of dumping can only reflect foreign market distortions and thus ignoring alternative causes of the pricing behaviour it targets, the anti-dumping law routinely punishes foreign firms for normal commercial conduct.

Price Differences and Sanctuary Markets

The lack of connection between affirmative dumping determinations and evidence of sanctuary markets is not surprising. The methodological flaws in pure price-to-price comparisons, compounded by the practice of using both price-to-price and cost-based comparisons in a single case, can result in findings of dumping even when there is no real pattern of international price differences. Furthermore, even when anti-dumping investigations do stumble onto cases of actual price discrimination, they are incapable of distinguishing between those that reflect the existence of a sanctuary market and those that are attributable to normal commercial factors. There are in fact many unexceptionable business reasons for charging more in one market than in another, and the persistence of those price differences over time by no means proves that the high-price market is closed.

International price differences can arise when a firm's status differs between national markets. A consumer goods firm may enjoy brand recognition in its home market that allows it to command a premium price; while abroad its brand name may be less valuable. Similarly, a producer goods firm may have built a reputation at home as a reliable supplier of high-quality products, while remaining relatively an unknown one in foreign markets. Or it may have carefully cultivated long-term business relationships with its domestic customers, while serving export markets on more of a spot-market basis. In all of those situations, the firm is exposed to greater pricing pressure abroad than at home and consequently will be forced to accept a lower price on its export sales.

Price differences can also result when the market structures or conditions in which a firm must operate vary from country to country. For example, market concentration may be higher in the firm's home market than abroad, and pricing pressures may consequently be less severe. Or numerical market concentration may have nothing to do with it; the vagaries of business culture and market history may combine to render a firm's home market less prone to aggressive price-cutting than a particular export market.

The resulting price differences across national markets in these examples reflect purely commercial factors and have nothing to do with government intervention or sanctuary markets.

Sales Below Cost and Market Distortions

Just as price discrimination can reflect the existence of market distortions, so can below-cost pricing be associated with 'abnormal' market behaviour. First, sales below marginal cost generally do not make commercial sense. While sales above marginal cost (but below full unit cost) at least make some contribution to recovering sunk costs, sales below marginal cost only compound total losses and therefore are almost always to be avoided. Likewise, firms cannot normally sell below full unit costs for a protracted period of time. Over the long term, chronic loss-making firms cannot attract the capital needed to stay in business. In these scenarios, firms exhibiting a pattern of making losses—whether of the acute, marginal cost variety or the chronic, below-unit-cost variety—may be benefiting from some form of government intervention that allows them to ignore normal market signals.

The usual reason for sales at a loss is nothing other than a normal, healthy, competitive marketplace. In the United States, for example, of the 4.47 million US corporations that filed tax returns in 1995, only 2.46 million—or 55 per cent—reported any net income.[14] Even the mightiest corporations are not immune from red ink. Looking back a few years, General Motors lost money three years in a row during 1990-1992, with accumulated pre-tax losses of $11.4 billion in that period. IBM posted two straight years of negative earnings in 1992 and 1993, racking up a staggering $17.8 billion of pre-tax losses—14 cents in the red for every dollar of sales.[15]

Sales at a loss can indicate all kinds of normal market phenomena. Companies that are going out of business generally leave a trail of red ink on the way out. Other times, losses are only temporary, as

14. US Bureau of the Census, *Statistical Abstract of the United States*: 1998, Table 863, p. 544.

15. Financial information taken from companies' 10-K reports.

companies make mistakes or business conditions deteriorate; companies can get back in the black by correcting errors and riding out the storm. During down periods, it may make good business sense to go on producing at a loss instead of cutting back production. For example, there may be long-term strategic benefits that accompany a certain market position (and market share); staying the market leader through a temporary downturn may maximise long-term profitability.

Also, if a downturn is seen as too temporary to justify permanent capacity cutbacks, it may pay to continue producing instead of allowing capacity to go idle. Here the distinction between marginal and sunk costs, or their real-world equivalents of variable and fixed costs, is crucial. If a company can continue to produce and sell goods above variable costs, it can at least make some contribution to fixed costs—costs that would be incurred even if those goods had not been produced. Under these conditions—which are typical for industries that face cyclical peaks and troughs of demand—continuing to produce and sell minimises total losses during the downturn.

For young companies, losses are not just common; they are the norm. Investment must come first, followed (eventually, if all goes well) by returns on that investment. In these circumstances, even fast-growing companies can generate significant red ink. Meanwhile, for established companies, losses are common on new products. By virtue of the well-known phenomenon of the 'learning curve', production costs tend to decline in line with cumulative production volume. Knowing this, businesses often price new goods below full current cost in order to increase sales volumes and accelerate passage down the learning curve. Such a strategy is intended to maximise profitability over the full life cycle of the product.

Eventually, of course, companies must turn a profit on their overall operations if they are to stay in business. Likewise, specific products must generally earn a profit sooner or later or else be dropped from a company's business line. There are, however, important exceptions. On some products, companies can lose money indefinitely; indeed, under certain conditions they may be well advised to do so.

For example, a multi-product firm may intentionally charge a money-losing price for one good to encourage higher sales of another good. Such a 'cross-subsidisation' strategy, if successful, can actually maximise overall firm profits.

Selling below full unit costs may also make sense in the case of so-called co-products or joint products—two or more different goods that are produced simultaneously in the same manufacturing process. Examples include different cuts of meat from the same animal, different ores extracted in the same mining operation, different chemicals produced by the same reaction, and products of varying quality produced in the same manufacturing batch. For those types of products, some allocation of shared manufacturing costs among the various joint products is necessary for cost-accounting purposes. Depending on how costs are allocated, a given co-product may show a profit or a loss.

In sum, sales below cost can mean many things other than the presence of government-caused market distortions. The anti-dumping law, however, completely ignores this possibility. When below-cost sales do end up getting caught in the wide net thrown in constructed-value and NME cases, the DOC's calculation methodologies fail to distinguish between normal commercial losses and those that point to the existence of government interventionism. As a result, anti-dumping law too often penalises normal commercial practices having nothing to do with anyone's definition of unfair trade.

For the existence of below-cost sales to raise any serious question of government interventionism, the losses must either be acute (i.e., sales must be below variable costs) or chronic (i.e., losses must persist for a period of years).

For chronic losses, the period investigated by the DOC in anti-dumping cases is only 12 months. Consequently, the DOC lacks the evidentiary record to determine whether a company's losses are abnormally persistent. Because the DOC does not take a longer view, it cannot determine whether losses reflect a temporary market downturn or business reversal, or whether they flow from a conscious growth-oriented strategy for a new company or a new product. Likewise, anti-dumping investigations develop no evidentiary record for determining whether acute or chronic losses, to the extent they exist, have a reasonable commercial explanation.

Most fundamental, the DOC does not examine whether the supposedly below-cost US sales it identifies are in any way connected with government interventionism in the home market. There is no investigation of whether trade barriers or other restrictions on competition create a domestic sanctuary market that bankrolls losses abroad; nor of whether the foreign producer receives government grants, soft loans, special tax breaks, preferential access to credit on non-commercial terms, or any other form of assistance that supports its loss-making operations; nor of whether there are basic structural flaws in a country's economic policy that impede normal market responses to losses.

Conclusion

The anti-dumping law is defended as a remedy for market distortions caused by foreign government policies. Yet in actual practice, the methods of determining dumping under the law fail, repeatedly and at multiple levels, to distinguish between normal commercial pricing practices and those that reflect market-distorting government policies.

As a result, the anti-dumping law as it currently exists routinely punishes normal competitive business practices—practices commonly engaged in by American companies at home and abroad. It is therefore not the case that the law guarantees a level playing field for American companies and their foreign competitors. On the contrary, it actively discriminates against foreign goods by subjecting them to requirements not applicable to American products.

An anti-dumping law that actually did target government caused market distortions would look very different from the law in its present form. Bringing the reality of anti-dumping practice into line with the rhetoric of anti-dumping supporters would require dramatic reforms. Such reform faces formidable obstacles. Use of anti-dumping laws around the world is widespread and growing; and wherever those laws operate, the protectionist *status quo* enjoys the support of entrenched bureaucracies and import-competing corporate interests. In the United States in particular, energetic and well-organised protectionist lobbies have mobilised nearly overwhelming political support for their position on anti-dumping issues. As a result, for many years the world's most powerful country and leader of the multilateral trading system has stood as the principal opponent of meaningful changes in anti-dumping rules.

Of all the obstacles hindering anti-dumping reform, however, none is greater than ignorance. Failure to understand how anti-dumping laws actually operate in practice—and how they fail so spectacularly to do what their supporters say they are supposed to do—lies at the root of much of the resistance to anti-dumping reform. Many supporters of the anti-dumping *status quo* honestly believe that these laws in their present form are necessary to combat unfair trading practices and thereby ensure a level playing field. If those supporters fully understood the reality of contemporary anti-dumping practice—if they understood how frequently trade-restrictive measures are inflicted on normal, healthy competition—their opposition to needed reforms would likely soften.

Of course, protectionist interests support the anti-dumping *status quo* so fervently precisely because of its flaws. Their goal is to squelch foreign competition in whatever way they can, and the anti-dumping law in its current form has proved very handy indeed. And because of ignorance about the law's complex workings, protectionist interests are able to cloak their special pleading in the high-minded rhetoric of fairness and concern for a level playing field. If they were forced to defend the *status quo* honestly, for the protectionist scam that it is, they would find it much harder to win adherents to their cause. Accordingly, education and clarification should be the top priorities of those advocating anti-dumping reform.

6

Anti-Dumping in the European Union

FREDRIK ERIXON

Introduction

Trade policy moves in mysterious ways. Since the late 18th century, indeed, perhaps even longer, there has been ample evidence of the economic and political benefits of free trade. Equally, the evidence of the failures of trade protectionism has been at the centre stage of the policy debate for the same period. Yet countries and politicians have time and again succumbed to protectionism. As Ulysses in the great Homer classic, politicians have listened to the fatal siren calls of protectionism, although being in full knowledge of that free trade and international economic integration is a superior choice.

The noble idea of unilateral free trade, the governing principle of the international economy in the late 19th century, was punctuated in the mid-war period. The attempt to restore the pre-1914 order after the First World War had failed bitterly, already in the 1920s, and many countries started to increase the tariff lines and broadly developed a 'beggar-thy-neighbour' policy poisoning international economic integration. In 1930, the United States introduced the notorious Smooth-Hawley Tariff Act and raised the level of tariff protection from 38 to 52 per cent. A few months later Australia, Canada, Cuba, France, Italy, Spain, and New Zealand followed suit and before long Great Britain, the home of the tradition of unilateral free trade, put the final nail in the coffin by opting for import protection. Since then, trade policy has largely been governed by a multilateral organisation and by principles bordering to mercantilism. As economist Paul Krugman once described modern trade policy:

> To make sense of international trade negotiations, one needs to remember three simple rules about the objectives of negotiating countries:

1. Exports are good.
2. Imports are bad.
3. Other things equal, an equal increase in import and exports is good.

In other words, GATT-think is enlightened mercantilism.[1]

Following the principle of enlightened mercantilism, the process of trade liberalisation in the post-war period has turned into a game of concessions. The mechanism of reciprocity—'I do what you do'—has enforced the mercantilist notion of trade policy reforms and steered attention away from the true idea of free trade: unilateral trade liberalisation acknowledging that the home country would benefit from decreased trade protection regardless of other countries choices. Free trade is primarily about getting access to goods and services that other countries can produce more efficiently. Therefore, trade protections are more damaging for the importing country than for the exporting country.

The latest development in EU-China trade relations is a case in point. In June last year (2005), the EU and China agreed to introduce a new system of quotas for 10 categories of textile products that are exported from China to the European Union. This followed the expiry of the 10-year long quota period in the WTO Agreement on Textiles and Clothing (ATC). However, the EU, as well as other countries using trade protection to curb their textile imports, did not prepare for the end of the quota system and soon after the New Year (the quotas expired on January 1, 2005) the EU Commission and the Council of Ministers faced heavy lobbying from the textile-producing interest group, Euratex, arguing for new protection.

The EU Commission responded to their call by forcing China to an agreement curbing Chinese export of 10 categories of textiles to 2008. In all crucial respects, this is a measure similar to an import tariff in the European Union; the purpose and the effect of the export restraint is to lower the export of particular products from China to the EU.

Now, the question is why all this happened? EU consumers had clearly benefited from the new open trade regime; the cost of clothes

1. Krugman, Paul (1991). "The move towards free trade zones", in *Policy Implications of Trade and Currency Zones: A Symposium* sponsored by The Federal Reserve Bank of Kansas City.

had fallen significantly in this short period and was about to fall even further as new Chinese imports reached the market. In Sweden some financial analysts even voiced concerns about the rapidly falling prices of clothing and how that would strengthen general deflationary pressures and cause macroeconomic imbalances.

Fuelled by the rising export, Chinese companies, in their turn, had been able to expand the production of textiles. Despite this so-called win-win situation for China and Europe, the EU Commission pushed heavily for new trade protectionism, claiming that European producers needed more time to adjust to the new competition. Thus, the Commission branded the new protection as an attempt to "manage change and adjustment rather than manage trade".[2]

But this is not the full story, only the tip of the iceberg. The EU had started investigations to measure up possible efforts to limit Chinese exports under the Textiles Specific Safeguard Clause in China's WTO Accession Protocol. A process of WTO consultation had also been started. The EU was apparently in search of every accessible method to block rising imports from China. The main purpose was undoubtedly to lower the competition for European textile producers, but the EU also labelled these efforts as an attempt to protect, or rather stimulate, an idea of 'equal trading opportunities' for poor and emerging countries. China, the argument was, is too an efficient producer and 'take' European market shares from other exporting countries that are also poor and in need of export opportunities. Therefore, the EU argued for a development-oriented view on trade policies that promotes export from countries that are not sufficiently competitive.

Economics of Anti-Dumping

The new system of quotas is not directly an anti-dumping measure, but it is a safeguard provision and bears close resemblance to the motif of many anti-dumping actions initiated by the European Union. One particular resemblance is that this new voluntary export restraint, as most actions taken under the anti-dumping heading, has nothing to do with 'dumping' or 'unfair' trade at all.

---

2. EU Commission (2005). "EU-China textile agreement", 10 June, *Memo*/05/201, Brussels.

There are several categories of 'dumping' actions, procedures, and motivations.[3] Economists generally speak about three types of dumping motivations from an exporting company. First of all, there exists a market-expansion dumping that is based on differences in demand between two particular markets. After the Asian financial crisis in 1997-98, domestic demand in Southeast Asia declined sharply and since China did not devalue its currency, as many other countries in the region did at the time, the price of Chinese export rose sharply and had to be redirected to other markets, in particular to the US and the European Union. This example illustrates aspects of market expansion, but also leads us to another motivation for dumping, cyclical dumping. Cyclical dumping usually occurs when demand falls rapidly or when there is an oversupply of a particular product. Thirdly, economists identify state trading dumping when a non-market economy creates, deliberately or not, an oversupply that subsequently is dumped on a market.

None of these motivations for dumping do generally cause trouble in trade relations. But in combination with other measures, they can result in situations that clearly hinder a free and fair trading order based on the principles of market economy. Two practices are of particular concern.

A company can sell their products in export markets at very low prices in order to obtain monopoly power by effectively making it impossible for competitors to stay in the market. To proponents of anti-dumping actions, this is allegedly a normal procedure in many markets and distorts not only trade but also economic efficiency in other ways. Once the predatory company has obtained monopoly power it can raise prices and profits. The company is not any longer constrained by normal market competition from other competitors.

This seems to be a situation where consumers clearly stand to loose from unfair trading practices. However, the case for anti-dumping measures to curb the behaviour of predatory companies is not as clear-cut as many assumes.

The sheer presence of a monopoly situation does not necessarily translate into rising prices. A monopolist faces competition from other products that can substitute the monopoly product and as long as

---

3. Barfield, Claude (2003). *High-tech Protectionism: The Irrationality of Anti-dumping laws*, Washington, DC, American Enterprise Institute.

there are no legal restrictions to enter a particular market, there is always a possibility of other companies entering the market, if the monopoly company raise prices and increase profits. This is, *mutatis mutandis*, the prime explanation to why monopolies in most circumstances occur only temporarily and why it is difficult to maintain price hikes. As have been shown by economist William Baumol and others, the presence of free entry and exit in a market tempers the predatory ambitions of monopolists.[4]

To be a successful strategy, predatory dumping moreover requires a few additional prerequisites. The predatory company needs a large market share at home that is protected, or in other ways function as a sanctuary market, and must have the possibility to obtain large market shares in another country. In case there are several competing companies in the home market they must in some way collude if they should be able to keep high prices after the companies in the foreign market have been driven out.

The second concern is similar to the market-expansion dumping discussed above but is not primarily about gaining control over a foreign market. Rather it is based on a situation where a company has a protected home market and compete in an industry with typical economies of scale characteristics.[5] If a company has access to both a home and a foreign market it can divide costs between these two locations and thus gets a cost advantage over a company from another market that is not able or prohibited to access the first company's home market. This 'strategic' dumping will sooner or later result in increased market power for the company with a cost advantage and, subsequently, price hikes and lowered economic efficiency.

These two concerns of the effects of dumping is part and parcel of the rhetoric of anti-dumping actions, in the European Union as well as in other countries. However, it is rarely observed that a government institution or agency provides sufficient evidence to prove that market-expansion dumping or strategic dumping really exists and that it lowers the welfare of consumers. Of greater concern to the world trading community is that few countries today, the EU in particular, bothers to investigate in detail whether a particular situation really is based on dumping and if it causes harm to consumers.

---

4. Baumol, William (1982). "Contestable Market: An Uprising in the Theory of Industry Structures", *American Economic Review* 72.
5. Economies of scale mean falling marginal costs of production.

Anti-Dumping Policy and Actions in the European Union

The EU rules to tackle dumping dates back to the earliest days of the community. Following the completion of the Uruguay Round, a new set of rules came into force on January 1, 1995 that replaced the old regulation. A few changes were also made in 1996 that are of importance to the procedure of investigating and deciding whether anti-dumping actions are called for or not.

The Commission is responsible for investigating complaints from parties allegedly harmed by dumping from third-country firm and thus also responsible for assessing whether the complaints are justified. In addition, the Commission can also impose provisional measures and in some cases also definitive measures (if it concerns coal and steel products). However, as a general rule it is the Council of Ministers that decides upon definite anti-dumping actions. In other words, it is a forum of elected politicians that decides whether anti-dumping duties should be imposed.

The European Community rules for anti-dumping provide for the imposition of anti-dumping duties when the following conditions are met:[6]

i) *A Finding of Dumping*: The export price at which the product is sold on the Community market is shown to be lower than the price on the producer's home market.

ii) *A Material Injury to Community Industry*: The imports have caused or threaten to cause damage to a substantial segment of the industry within the European Community, such as a loss of market share, reduced prices for producers and resulting pressure on production, sales, profits, productivity, etc.

iii) *The Interest of the Community*: The costs for the Community of taking measures must not be disproportionate to the benefits.

In other words, an industry, a company or a group of companies in the European Union that considers import from a non-EU country to be dumped and causing material injury to the industry, can submit a complaint to the Commission, directly or through its national government. Within 45 days the Commission will then examine the complaint, consult the member states and subsequently decide

6. EU Commission (2005). *Anti-dumping: Protection Against Dumped Imports*, Brussels, EU Commission.

whether or not there is sufficient evidence to merit a formal investigation. If there is no evidence or, *nota bene*, if the complainants do not represent at least 25 per cent of the total EU production in question, the complaint shall be rejected.

A formal investigation normally does not take more than a year. During that time period the Commission may impose provisional duties. These duties cannot exceed the difference between the price on the home market and the export price on the EU market. Furthermore, they are not allowed to last more than nine months. After nine months, the Council must decide whether the anti-dumping actions should be prolonged. If a third country consider an imposed anti-dumping in the EU to be unfair or not in tune with WTO agreements, they can turn to the WTO dispute settlement mechanism or challenge the anti-dumping action in the European Court of First Instance.

Anti-dumping measures are, as in other WTO member countries, basically governed by the WTO rules in GATT Article VI, and are embodied in various forms. An *ad valorem* duty is a fixed percentage of the CIF prices before payment of customs duty. A specific duty is a fixed amount per unit imported. There is also a duty based on an amount equal to the difference between the price of a product at the European Community frontier and a fixed price established by the EC Commission.

Earlier, price undertakings were a common result of an anti-dumping procedure, in particular between China and the European Union. A price undertaking is a voluntary price hike by the exporter, in other words, a voluntary method to restrain exports. The rules for price undertakings in the European Union are not well articulated, leaving a considerable discretion to the EU Commission and the Council of Ministers. However, since the 1990s the EU has been much less inclined to accept offers of price undertakings from foreign companies and instead opted for *ad valorem* duties. Up to 1990 about 30 per cent of all anti-dumping cases ended in a price undertaking, but since then the role of price undertaking has diminished.[7] This is a good development. A legal-based trading order should rely on duties rather than voluntary price undertakings. Moreover, duties are more

7. Belderbos, René, Hylke, Vandenbussche and Reinhilde, Veugelers (1999). "Anti-dumping Duties, Undertakings, and Foreign Direct Investment in the EU", *Mimeo*, Leuven, Catholic University of Leuven.

likely to result in so-called anti-dumping jumping—substituting exports with foreign direct investments (FDI), instead of exporting a particular product to the EU a company invests in production facilities in the EU—which subsequently promotes higher price competition within the EU.[8]

Two crucial aspects of the EU anti-dumping procedure need to be highlighted. The first aspect concerns the method of deciding definite anti-dumping measures. Decisions are usually taken (unless it concerns coal and steel products) by the Council of Ministers, which is a forum of elected politicians. The sheer idea, or presence, of an elected body deciding matters concerning compliance of rules is not only surprising but also subject to criticism. It is a practice that is arguably not in tune with democratic ideas and praxis; elected politicians shall decide rules but should not be monitoring or policing them. In addition, such a procedure opens the whole process of anti-dumping impositions to other considerations than the pure economical concerns stated in the Community rules.

It is obvious from a political economy perspective that this method invites political concerns to be taken into consideration; representatives of a country or a region with companies that could stand to benefit from an anti-dumping duty have a political interest to support an anti-dumping petition whether it is in the general welfare interest of the EU or not. The risk of being faced with heavy opposition from domestic interest groups is often sufficient to close the proceedings for economic rationality. In particular, if a decision is close to a parliamentary election, then the general interest is easily suffered on the altar of a local interest in conflict with the public good. Political economy considerations are also strengthened by the lack of voting transparency in the Council. Although it is often leaked how a particular country has voted in the Council, votes are in principle a secret and not subject to public scrutiny.

In 2004, the voting rules were also changed in a way that leads to a bias in favour of imposing anti-dumping measures. Before the change anti-dumping duties could only be made definite after the Council of Ministers had approved it in a simple majority vote where

8. Of course, anti-dumping jumping depends on the possibility for the exporting firm to transfer the cost advantage to the FDI receiving country. If that is possible, a price undertaking, which is a price fixing arrangement, is more likely to favour export rather than FDI.

abstentions counted as a vote against imposing an anti-dumping duty. Since March 2004, however, abstentions count as a vote in favour of imposing an anti-dumping measure. Opposing an anti-dumping action has to be a proactive choice rather than the other way round. In other words, the 'default position' is in favour of protectionism.

The second aspect concerns the evidence in favour of anti-dumping actions. As in the United States, the ground for anti-dumping actions is, besides material injury to EU industry, an observation of a so-called dumping margin, a difference in price between sales in the home market and the export price on EU markets.[9] True, there is also sort of a 'Community Interest Clause' pointing to the need for a general welfare interest in the EU to be present in order to legitimise anti-dumping actions. But that principle is rarely tested and, do not generally govern EU policies.

The methods of calculating the dumping margin can in formal investigations be very complicated and difficult to understand even for experienced analysts of anti-dumping policies. But the major concern here is principally not the merits of various methods of investigating dumping practices; the concern is rather on the nature of the definition of dumping. Primarily because a lower price in the EU market than in, say, the Indian market is not an injury to consumers. On the contrary, if a foreign company sells its product at a lower price in the EU than it does at home it is rather beneficial for the EU consumers. In particular because the export price of a foreign company is lower than the price of the domestic EU producer (anti-dumping actions do not concern foreign companies that sell at higher prices than EU producers in the EU market).

What is more, the sheer presence of a difference in price between an exporter's home market and the EU market does not imply a presence of dumping, injury to domestic producers or predatory pricing practices hurting consumers.[10] In fact, a price difference alone does not mean anything of that kind. Price differences are very normal parts of an international economy and often reflect market differences. If prices were not to reflect market differences, differences in demand as well as differences on the supply side, it would not only be a static

9. For a thorough and detailed description of the US anti-dumping procedures, see Brink, Lindsey and Daniel Ikenson (2003). *Anti-dumping Exposed: The Devilish Details of Unfair Trade Law*, Washington, DC, Cato Institute.

10. Here predatory pricing refers to pricing below the marginal cost of production.

loss to consumers but also hamper natural market responses and the dynamic development of the market.

Admittedly, the philosophy of anti-dumping actions is partly intended to be in opposition to basic economics. But the practice of anti-dumping has moved away from its original purposes and is now largely used as a common protectionist measure to stifle competition, whether the competition is unfair or not. A closer look on how the European Union is acting in the realm of anti-dumping will provide ample evidence of the political economy of anti-dumping actions.

The European Union is however not the most notorious user of anti-dumping action. The United States has for many decades been the main perpetrator of the use of anti-dumping measures and continues to be the country with the highest number of anti-dumping measures in place. During 1995-2000, the average number of anti-dumping measures in place was 323 for the United States, followed by the European Union (143), Canada (88), Mexico (84), and South Africa (59). The corresponding figure for the world total was 976.[11]

This definitely testifies a sharp increase in the use of anti-dumping measures. Anti-dumping cases numbered 2113 between 1990 and 1999, which is an increase about a third from the 1401 cases between 1980 and 1989.[12] Another major trend in the use of anti-dumping measure is the rapid rise of anti-dumping actions taken by developing countries. Formerly a practice mainly employed by developed countries, it is now used by many developing countries as well—Brazil, China, India and South Africa in particular.[13] In only six years (1995-2000), South Africa's share of the number of anti-dumping measures in place rose from 2 per cent to 10 per cent. During the same period, India's share of the world total grew even faster, from 1.5 per cent in 1995 to 9 per cent in 2000.

This development seems set to continue. In 2003-04, Brazil, China, India and South Africa jointly accounted for 32 per cent of all new initiations of anti-dumping investigations. True, most developing countries have lately followed the global trend of a small but at least

11. Lindsey and Ikenson, *op cit.*, p. 107.
12. Erixon, Fredrik (2001). *A Radical Agenda for the Millennium Round*, Stockholm, Timbro.
13. National Board of Trade (2005). *The Use of Anti-dumping in Brazil, China, India and South Africa—Rules, Trends and Causes*, Stockholm, National Board of Trade.

observable fall in the number of new anti-dumping investigations and final anti-dumping measures, but developing countries continue to increase their share in the total number of anti-dumping investigations and actions.

There are various explanations to the trend of increased use of anti-dumping actions in the developing world. Part of the explanation is that developing countries have generally gained strength—in world trade policy affairs as well as in their share of the world trade volume—and now reciprocate, or perhaps retaliate, with the same unfriendly measures.[14]

Another explanation takes stock against the trend of trade liberalisations during the last decades; as tariffs have been lowered, quotas expired and developing countries generally opened up their economies to the world, anti-dumping initiations have been one course of action still open for general protectionism. The same is true on the global level: the rise in the number of anti-dumping measures is closely related to the decline in tariff protections.

Put differently, the rise in the number of anti-dumping filings in the developing world seems not to be related to any rise in dumping practices, by firms in developed countries or their counterparts in the developing world.

The EU's share in the anti-dumping cases has declined with the rise of the developing country share. As shown in Figure 6.1, EU represented in 2003 approximately 5 per cent of all anti-dumping actions taken. Measured differently, as the share of the total anti-dumping measures in place, the EU represented 14 per cent during the period 1995-2000.[15]

In the last five years, the number of investigations and impositions of definite anti-dumping measures have also declined. As shown in Table 6.1, the number of new investigations in 2004 was slightly higher than the average for the last five years, but looking at the trend it is observed that the number of investigations is declining.

---

14. National Board of Trade, *ibid.*

15. Lindsey and Ikenson, *op. cit.*

Figure 6.1

EU Share of Anti-Dumping Actions (%)

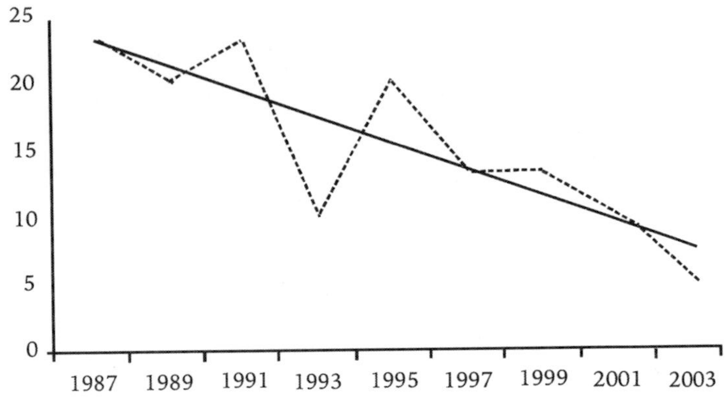

Source: WTO.

Table 6.1

New Investigations and Impositions of Definite Anti-Dumping Measure (2000-2004)[16]

Year	*2000*	*2001*	*2002*	*2003*	*2004*	*Average*
Investigations	31	33	23	8	29	24.8
Impositions	51	12	28	5	11	21.4

Table 6.2 exhibits how new investigations by the EU are largely about exports from developing countries. In 2004, 86 per cent of all new investigations concerned exports from developing countries. In 2003, the share was as high as 100 per cent. This is not a new development. For decades, anti-dumping investigations from the EU —and the United States—have mainly focused on developing country exports.

16. European Commission (2004). *Anti-dumping, Anti-subsidy, Safeguard,* Statistics Covering 2004, Brussels, European Commission.

Table 6.2

New Investigations Initiated by Country of Export (2000-2004)[17]

Year	*2000*	*2001*	*2002*	*2003*	*2004*
Developing Country	29	32	19	8	25
Developed Country	2	1	4	0	4
Developing Country (Share of new investigations, %)	94	97	79	100	86

There are of course several explanations to this phenomenon. Some developing countries are non-market economies that employ market practices that are not conducive to the idea of free trade (defined here as the absence of state intervention). But the main explanation to the high share of developing countries in new EU investigations is the cost advantage in developing countries. The cost of labour is lower in developing countries than the same in the EU, which gives producers in developing countries an advantage in labour intensive production. Thus, companies from developing countries can overall keep lower market prices for their products. And when the competition is generally tougher in the EU market than in a developing country, the exporting company can or even must keep lower prices in the EU market than in their home market.

Again, this practice has virtually nothing to do with harmful dumping or 'unfair' trade but is a normal market practice. Similarly, blocking these companies' export opportunities by imposing anti-dumping duties, or forcing them to price undertakings, has nothing to do with protecting a fair trading order or protecting consumers. It is sheer protectionism.

The European Union and Anti-Dumping: In Lieu of Conclusion

Factors of political economy can explain much of the use of anti-dumping measures, in the European Union as well as in other countries. This does not mean that all anti-dumping actions are influenced by political considerations. As shown in a few recent research papers, the role of political influence in anti-dumping decisions are easy to observe in the EU as well as in the US, but it

17. European Commission (2004), *ibid.*

is not the only factor explaining the use of anti-dumping measures.[18] Some cases are addressing dumping activities that are outright abuses of free trade. Another set of explanations, to some extent also taking stock against political economy factors, seems to concern macroeconomic variables and their influence on changes in prices. For example, if an economy is expanding there is likely to be an increase in demand. This would, *ceteris paribus*, likely to raise the price of exporter's products and thus reduce the likelihood of dumping. Inversely, in a recession, where demand is falling, the price of the export product is likely to fall as the exporter try to retain the market share, and this increase the likelihood of dumping.

Changes in the relative price of a country's currency can also have the same effects and research seems to suggest that appreciations of the real exchange rate in the EU have a positive impact on the openings of anti-dumping procedures.[19]

Although not being the most notorious user of anti-dumping measures, the European Union has to take a lot of the blame for the contagion of anti-dumping measures that we have witnessed over the last decades. In particular, since the EU has been prone to use anti-dumping measures to protect domestic producers from fair competition—some even suggest that EU started this trend (especially anti-dumping actions against China, the country faced the highest number of anti-dumping actions).

In principal, the EU is in favour of a reform of the anti-dumping practices and a WTO reform. However, that does not necessarily mean that the EU will stop using measures to curb exports from low-cost countries. As the recent developments in EU-China trade relations have shown, there are other methods to use if a country is really interested in diluting free trade. To manage change and adjustment, and to promote a 'redistribution' of trading shares for several countries in the developing world, were the arguments used by the EU Commission to defend the new quotas against Chinese textile exports.

This is perhaps a change in rhetoric, but not in practice.

---

18. Sadni-Jallab, Mustapha, René Sandretto and Robert Feinberg (2005). "An Empirical Analysis of US and EU Anti-dumping Initiation and Decision", *Mimeo*; and Douglas, Irwin (2005). "The Rise of Anti-dumping in Historical Perspective", *IMF Working Paper*, WP/05/31, Washington, DC, International Monetary Fund.

19. Sadni-Jallab, Mustapha *et al.*, *op cit.*

7

Why is China the World's Number One Anti-Dumping Target?

YUEFEN LI[1]

Introduction

The first anti-dumping investigation against China was launched by the European Community in 1979, immediately after China started opening its economy to the outside world. Since then, the filing of contingent protection measures targeted at China have proliferated at a rapid pace, with anti-dumping actions far more prevalent than other measures such as safeguards. In the 1980s, anti-dumping cases against China averaged 6.3 per year. The number increased to 30.3 per year in the 1990s.[2] From 1996 up to the present day, China has ranked first in the world in anti-dumping investigations and final measures against its exports.

The cost of anti-dumping activities against Chinese exports is quite high. From 1979 up to October 2002, 33 countries have initiated 544 anti-dumping and safeguard cases and measures against Chinese exports affecting more than 4,000 products with a total value of around US$ 16 billion (People's Daily, 2003). However, this amounted to only about 5 per cent of China's total exports, and was not extensive enough to cripple the economy.

An analysis follows on the major factors contributing to China's position as number one target of anti-dumping investigations in the world over the past consecutive few years.

1. The opinions expressed in this chapter are those of the author and do not necessarily reflect the views of UNCTAD. The chapter is a shorter version of a study published by the author in the UNCTAD book entitled *China in a Globalizing World (2005)*, Geneva.

2. "China is facing non-tariff barrier", For details see *www.cei.gov.cn*.

External Factors

Anti-Dumping Laws could be used to Benefit Multinational Enterprises and Victimise Late Industrialisers

As laws are not amended as frequently as developments take place, it is not uncommon for them to be manipulated and abused by contemporaries. However, when laws are too outdated, they may give rise to incidences of running against the very principles on which the law was introduced.

Many countries have amended their anti-dumping (AD) laws in recent years. The WTO Agreement on Anti-dumping was endorsed in 1994, only a relatively short time ago. However, some of the basic economic assumptions of international trade conducted in the 18th century are still the cornerstone of the AD laws. That is what a recent study describes as a "residency-based view of trade", which means that exports are goods and services leaving a nation's borders, regardless of nationality and ownership of producers and service-providers involved, while imports are the mirror of exports (Farrell *et al.*, 2005). However, these basic assumptions no longer apply to a large part of international trade because of the tremendous changes that have occurred since the days of barter trade and the time when the first anti-dumping laws were introduced. Multinational enterprises (MNEs) have increasingly begun to offshore their production activities and trade between affiliates and their parent companies have mushroomed.

A significant proportion of the goods and services exported from a country do not really belong to that particular country. With FDI, companies no longer need to cross national borders to sell their products. A volume of cross-border trade directly associated with the determination of dumping action no longer accurately reflects actual commercial activities between two trading nations. Not to take these changes and factors into consideration in AD laws may result in the unwelcoming outcome of not meeting the intended purpose of legislators when they enacted the law. Anti-dumping duties were conceived in Canada at the beginning of the 19th century with the intention of maintaining a 'level playing field' for domestic industries whose activities essentially took place within national frontiers. Subsequently, they were extended to cover transactions from outside the national borders. However, as pointed out by Richard J. Pierce Jr.

(1999:2), globalisation and the rise of MNEs have meant that in many cases anti-dumping laws have been administered and manipulated to "facilitate the formation, maintenance, and enforcement of cartels".

One common feature of anti-dumping laws/agreements is that they have sufficient loopholes to allow MNEs to use them to squeeze out efficient new market rivals. This is one important reason why major newly-industrialising economies (NIEs) experienced a hard time when they were the targets of contingent protection measures; this came at a period when they underwent fast economic growth and foreign trade expansion, which quite often forced them to set up foreign direct investment (FDI) operations abroad. China has entered such a period, but has not yet developed the capacity to engage in large scale FDI to jump anti-dumping activities.

The internationalisation and segmentation of production chains and the rise of MNEs have rendered anti-dumping laws antiquated. On the whole, anti-dumping laws/agreements have placed countries that have few MNEs and countries that are new entrants to the global market at a very disadvantageous position. MNEs are demanders of export prices and also have the capability to collude against a particular product from a developing country; they do so by using contingent protection measures, creating instability and uncertainty for their exports such as reductions in trade volumes, losing market shares for their goods and, in some cases, withdrawing from the market totally. MNEs have used anti-dumping measures as an instrument to strengthen their monopoly (Messerlin, 2002).

The costs of anti-dumping measures on the domestic economies of the targeted countries in terms of financial losses and human suffering when workers are laid off are much larger for developing countries than in the case of industrial countries. For the initiating countries, the protection it affords its domestic producers is limited. It is true that a number of developing countries, including China, have also become major initiators of anti-dumping investigations; however, more often than not, this was because domestic industries find it hard to adjust to a highly competitive environment. Without large MNEs, they are not in a position to use anti-dumping to create a monopoly in a certain market.

Dramatic changes have taken place in the global economy since the promulgation of the first anti-dumping law in Canada. The rise of MNEs and progress made in technology and communication has fundamentally changed the landscape of global production supply chains. Production is now globalised and segmented. Component and service inputs and assembly operations involved in the production of a traded product can now take place in different countries. The growing integration of national economies, a process known as globalisation, is mainly coordinated by MNEs through FDI and, to a lesser extent, by other contractual arrangements. An important part of FDI is market oriented which means that affiliates of MNEs sell products directly to host-country markets, thus jumping both tariff, non-tariff barriers including anti-dumping concerns. This renders outdated the concept of trade balance since it does not cover the goods and services sold by MNEs in FDI host countries, even though these can be very significant.

MNE affiliates in host countries are treated as residencies of these countries. Their local sales, regardless of whether they are goods or services, are not considered as exports and are therefore not included in the trade balance. In cases when these affiliates export goods and services produced in the FDI host countries to their home countries, they would be reflected in the trade balance as exports of the FDI host country to the MNE affiliates' home country. According to an article published by McCaughrin (2004) (Figure 7.1):

> Nearly three times as many goods are sold overseas by US foreign affiliates as by US exporters. Incorporating foreign affiliate sales reduces the US deficit by almost a full percentage point of GDP. US multinationals are not alone in relying on affiliates to distribute goods overseas. Japanese multinationals exported \$325bn of goods during the first three quarters of 2003. But on top of that, Japanese affiliates sold an additional \$287 bn of goods (excluding sales back to Japan) that are not captured in the trade balance.

So for the MNEs, in addition to the various incentives offered by the host countries, the goods and services sold directly in foreign markets by their affiliates are not included in the bilateral trade balance, thus minimising domestic political pressure on host countries to take contingent protection against them. This makes a major criteria to impose contingent protection such as 'material injury' to domestic producers, 'import surge' and 'market disruption' less relevant. Japanese FDI flows to the European Union and the United States in the 1980s were positively affected by the overall increase in the number of anti-dumping actions in the two jurisdictions. This may explain why Japan's position in the anti-dumping investigations league tables fell from its number one position for the period of 1981–1997 to the fourth position for the period of 1995-2001 (Zanardi, 2004). In addition, once production facilities have been set up in these jurisdictions, they can file anti-dumping petitions under local anti-dumping laws against foreign rivals. China, being a developing country, still relies heavily on exports to promote its economic development.

Figure 7.1

Sales of Services and Goods of United States Affiliates in China (1989–2001)

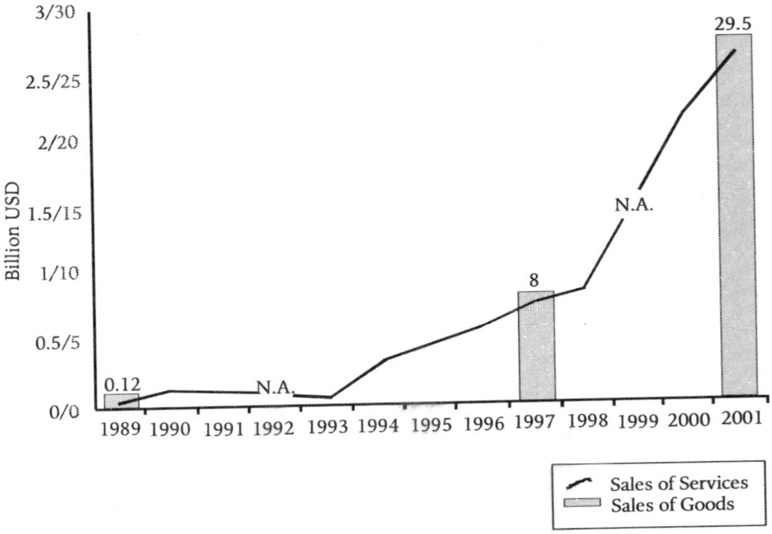

Sources: Bureau of Economic Analysis (*www.bea.doc.gov*).
Economic Policy Institute (*www.epinet.org*).

As MNEs have production facilities located in different parts of the world, they are also capable of dodging anti-dumping activities targeted at exports from their affiliates. For instance, if a MNE has had an affirmative anti-dumping ruling against products it has manufactured in China, the MNE could redirect the product to a market other than the one with anti-dumping restrictions in place against the product made in China. Meanwhile, its affiliate located in a third country can export the same product to the complaining country with a product originating from a country other than China. Thus, through trade diversion, the MNE could survive positive anti-dumping rulings without losing market share. In 2003, the United States threatened to levy dumping charges on some colour TV sets made in China. A company such as Philips exported large screen TVs assembled in China to the United States and its Chairman and Chief Executive said that the anti-dumping activity "do not affect Philips operations" as his company "could shift TV production to its Mexico plants" and export to the US market from there.

Another phenomenon, which goes hand in hand with globalisation and growing interdependence is that, so-called domestic industries are, in many cases, no longer purely domestic. They very often have similar and varied ties with MNEs, e.g., shareholding and contractual assembling operations. They can even sometimes be affiliates of MNEs based in a complaining country. Vested interests give rise to suspicions of collusion to snatch market share from competitors. One example is the anti-dumping investigation against Chinese colour TVs in the United States. As pointed out by the head of the International Brotherhood of Electrical Workers, the trade union supporting the anti-dumping filing, "the majority of TV manufacturing in the U.S. is multinational. There are very few American companies producing TVs."[3] Labour unions at Sanyo Manufacturing in Arkansas, Sharp Electronics in Tennessee and Toshiba America in New Jersey are all Japanese firms that have a part to play in the case against Chinese TV producers. Because of this, there has been "a widespread suspicion among the China industry that Japanese companies were behind the case (Yan, 2004)."

MNEs, through their affiliates, often collude with each other to squeeze out new foreign market entrants, particularly new and weak entrants from developing countries. According to Maur (1998: 17):

> ... collusion between firms operating in several countries and deciding to hit jointly a common foreign rival—especially when these firms do not occupy a dominant position in their respective markets could be another hypothesis for explaining multiple overseas petitions. We can imagine that MNE firms meeting in a specific market may agree to coordinate their strategies against a common rival. Some instances of 'echoing' could support that hypothesis.

---

3. See IBEW website: *http://www.ibew.org/stories/03journal/030708/p12b.htm*.

This explains why most NIEs are targets of anti-dumping activities or have experienced a period of intense trade friction with major industrialised countries. China is also going through a period of heavy reliance on foreign trade to promote economic growth and industrialisation. The following table on ratio of share of anti-dumping investigations and share of export value shows that China's ratio of share of anti-dumping investigations is very high in relation to its share of world trade (Table 7.1). This could support the hypothesis that it is a target of anti-dumping and that China is, in fact, faring worse than NIEs. According to its WTO accession agreement, China will continue to be treated as a non-market economy until 2016. China's non-market economy status makes it an even easier target of MNE collusion, as 'surrogate values' for anti-dumping ruling are always obtained from a third party in 'comparable market-economy countries'. MNEs sometimes succeeded in getting companies related to the enterprises in the complaining country to provide surrogate values. Several studies documented cases of collusion against Chinese exports (Maur, 1998).

Table 7.1

Ratio of Share of Anti-Dumping Investigations and Share of Export Value

Country	*Share of Anti-Dumping Investigations in Total World Investigations (Per Cent)*				*Export Share of Total World Exports (Per cent)*				*Ratio of Share of Anti-Dumping Investigations and the Share of Export Value*			
	A	B	C	D	A	B	C	D	A	B	C	D
China	4.15	10.97	13.59	9.40	1.45	2.36	4.00	2.44	2.86	4.65	3.40	3.85
Japan	8.88	5.88	4.42	6.50	6.92	8.68	6.98	7.74	1.28	0.68	0.63	0.84
Republic of Korea	5.16	6.89	7.96	6.58	1.46	2.17	2.51	2.03	3.53	3.18	3.17	3.24
Taiwan Province of China	4.06	4.60	5.25	4.58	1.20	2.15	2.14	1.84	3.58	2.14	2.45	2.49
United States	8.71	8.53	4.36	7.64	14.63	11.76	11.90	12.70	0.60	0.73	0.37	0.60

Sources: UN Comtrade Database; WTO Anti-dumping Gateway (*www.wto.org*); Zanardi (2002); UNCTAD calculations.

Note: A : 1981-1987 B : 1988-1998 C : 1998-2002 D : 1981-2002

MNEs are also capable of creating a dumping scenario to take advantage of a protected market after a positive ruling of dumping. There were cases when foreign firms chose to increase the likelihood that trade barriers would be erected against its own industry, as this could be an optimal strategy if the firm could then shift production to the protected country and tariff jump thereby giving them the edge over competing foreign firms unable to engage in FDI. The mechanism is a simple one. When MNEs spot a new efficient entrant to the market, they purposely reduce their sales in that market in order to fabricate a proof of injury in the investigation stage of an anti-dumping petition. Then, after anti-dumping restrictive measure forced the new rival to withdraw from the market, they would re-enter the much more protected market. This is a strategic way for MNEs to maximise their profit margin and optimise their monopoly.

Globalisation has hastened the growth of buyer-driven commodity chains that connect advanced country marketing or retail companies with contractors manufacturing in low-cost developing economies (Frenkel, 2001). Very often the lead firm is a brand name merchandiser or a large retailer in a developed country, which orchestrates the procurement, manufacture and marketing of products manufactured by contractors, and sub-contractors in developing countries. Because of China's cost advantages, in particular low labour cost, China has become an important downstream producer in these global commodity chains. However, one of the constant pressures facing those at the lower end of the commodity chain is the incessant demand by brand name merchandisers and large retail distributors for lower export prices. If these demands are not met the producers risk losing the contracts; and Chinese firms have little bargaining power as they depend on the demands of MNEs. As noted by Gereffi *et al.* (1999), the powerful influence of the lead firm in shaping contractor relations is indisputable.

By pressuring Chinese suppliers, these retailers and wholesalers may very well widen their profit margins. However, they also push Chinese suppliers into a very unpleasant anti-dumping petition. All the same, when it comes to anti-dumping investigations, the tendency would be to blame Chinese enterprises for taking away jobs of the complaining countries instead of wholesalers or retailers of the complaining country trying to optimise their bottom lines.

In a number of anti-dumping cases against Chinese enterprises, those enterprises involved were caught between the conflicts of the various domestic interests of the complaining country. Two recent anti-dumping cases inspired by the United States against Chinese wooden bedroom furniture and colour TV illustrate this. In the case for furniture, the United States Department of Commerce noted that the anti-dumping petition on Chinese wooden bedroom furniture has split the furniture manufacturing and retail industries as companies are taking sides in the political battle. The United States Furniture Retailer Association published an article on its website which reveals that the anti-dumping petition, to a large extent was a conflict between domestic forces (namely export interests *versus* import-competing interests) than a conflict between countries.[4]

The rise of MNEs and four decades of trade liberalisation also render anti-dumping ineffective in protecting domestic industries. Indeed, anti-dumping measures can cost exporters dearly and can even totally exclude them from a market as shown by the European Union anti-dumping rulings against Chinese colour TVs and bicycles. Because of this, anti-dumping has risen in prominence as an instrument for imposing import restrictions. However, trade diversion from other producers can fill the vacuum within a very short period of time. Modern technology and communication, and segmentation of the production chain can all in one way or another facilitate the process. So what 'the injured domestic producers' get from a positive ruling is mostly just a breathing space of very limited duration. On top of this, due to increasing interdependence, anti-dumping actions also have had a negative impact on other interest groups of the complaining country.

As demonstrated in the United States furniture case against China, wholesalers, retailers and wood exporters in the United States suffer at the same time as Chinese furniture manufacturers. The only beneficiaries are the United States furniture manufacturers. For exports with high import contents, the characteristic of Chinese exports, all of the parties involved in the production chain will, to some extent, be negatively affected by anti-dumping rulings. And as shown by the furniture case, more often than not, the type of trade restrictions seen today end up redistributing trade, disproportionately penalising one country while rewarding another, without necessarily achieving the original objective of protecting the industry intended.

---

4. Historical background: Chinese bedroom furniture imports and the US furniture industry. See for more detail *www.furnitureretailers.org*.

Trade Liberalisation, Contingent Protection and Newly Industrialising Economies

China's impressive expansion of international trade started during late 1970s, when two decades of trade liberalisation had already resulted in considerably lower tariff levels in many countries. Since then further deepening of trade liberalisation has reduced significantly the importance of tariff as a trade barrier. As anti-dumping activities can be invoked relatively easily and selectively compared to other trade measures, and as anti-dumping investigations, regardless of the nature of their final rulings, can lead to almost immediate loss of market share on the part of exporting countries, they have also become the most frequently used trade remedies. By the 1990s anti-dumping had become a major instrument of trade protection for developed countries. Since the WTO Agreements went into effect in 1995, this instrument has become increasingly popular in all countries. So while trade liberalisation opens doors for late industrialisers; anti-dumping, safeguard, and countervailing measures have also been used to deter or harass them, China in particular.

Both developed and developing country governments have been encouraging and supporting domestic producers to use anti-dumping as a mechanism to protect their markets. Developing countries started to enact anti-dumping laws and tried to raise awareness on anti-dumping practices. Developed countries have made anti-dumping activities user-friendlier. Some have even provided incentives to the users of anti-dumping measures. In the United States, amendments to anti-dumping law have made it easier for domestic firms to prove the existence of dumping, including extensions of the definition of 'less than fair value' to include both international price discrimination and sales below cost (Prusa and Skeath, 2002: 4). Moreover, the United States has one particular legislation, known as the Byrd Amendment, designed to give anti-dumping duties collected by the United States Customs Service to private companies that filed anti-dumping petitions. In the fiscal year 2003, United States Customs and Border Protection paid out US$190 million in Byrd Amendment claims.[5] It is a *de facto* subsidy to anti-dumping petitioners, as indicated in the WTO ruling in April 2004.

Given this kind of international environment at a time when China was going through fast trade expansion, it is not surprising that it has

5. See *www.cbp.gov/xp/cgov/import/add_cvd/cont_dump/cdsoa_03/* of the United States Customs and Border Protection agency.

become the world's number one target for anti-dumping activities. However, as we will see in the next section, China's specific trade and economic structure has also contributed to the skyrocketing of anti-dumping charges against its exports.

Domestic Factors Contributing to the Utilisation of Contingent Protection Measures against Chinese Exports

From 1978 to 2002, China's exports increased by around 12 per cent on a year-on-year basis—much higher than the world average (Figure 7.2). While it is not an unprecedented phenomenon, China's sharp increase of trade within a relatively short period of time is still quite remarkable. Not surprisingly, this event has given rise to increasing anti-dumping petitions. Currently, China's large bilateral trade surplus with the United States is a heated political topic in the United States and has led to allegations of currency manipulation and unfair trade practices. All this indicates that China has now entered a stage of intense trade frictions with some of its trading partners, as did Japan in the 1970s.

Figure 7.2

Trade Expansion in China (1982–2004)

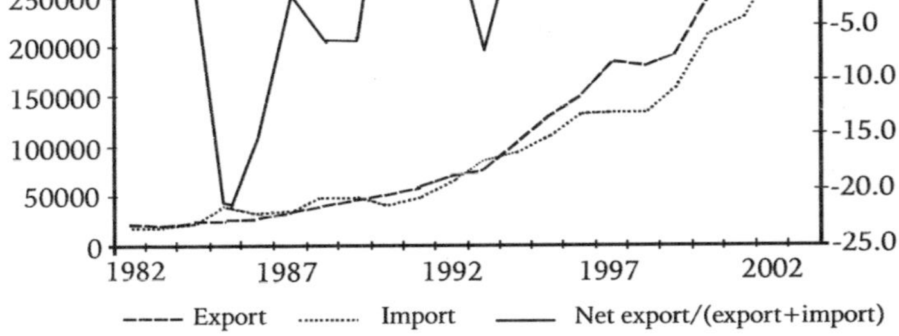

Source : IMF DOT, February 2005.

Note : Estimates for 2004 are based on the nine-month cumulative value of 2004 over the same period in 2003. Note on World Exports in EIU: "... in November 2004 (year-to-year) exports grew by 46 per cent."

China's trade structure also makes it an easy target of trade protectionist measures. Exports are highly concentrated to certain key destinations. Although great efforts have been made to diversify, progress has not been as fast as it could have been. The United States, Japan, European Union and Hong Kong (China) still account for 70 per cent of China's exports.[6] For example, 75 per cent of China's textile and apparel exports are concentrated in five markets, i.e. Hong Kong (China), Japan, the United States, the European Union and the Republic of Korea. Another example is furniture export. According to official statistics, China produced nearly US$20 billion worth of furniture in 2002, of which one-third was exported, half of it to the United States (China Daily, 2003). This high reliance on a few markets gives rise to higher anti-dumping pressure in these markets (see Figure 7.3).

Figure 7.3

Export Destinations of China

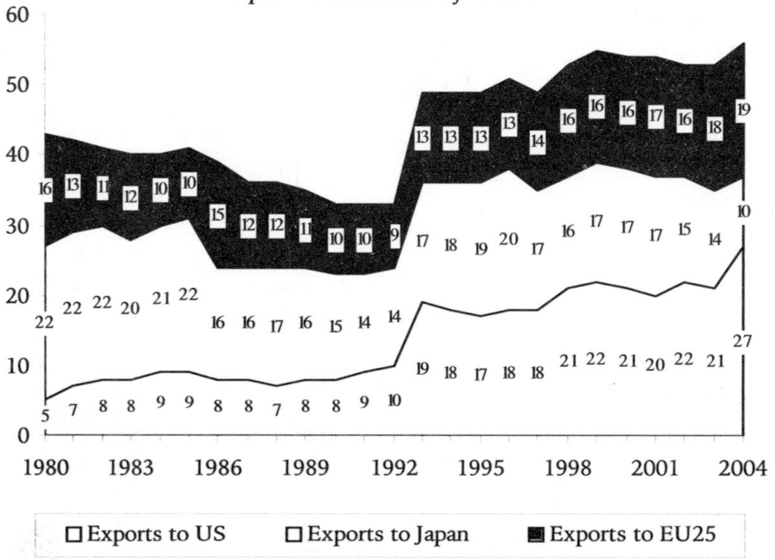

Source : IMF DOT February 2005.

Note : Estimates for 2004: based on the 9-month cumulative value of 2004 over same period in 2003 Note on WORLD exports in EIU: "...in November 2004 (year-to-year) exports grew by 46 per cent."

6. See for more details China Economic Information Network at *www.cei.gov.cn*.

As for export product categories, up to the first half of 1990s China's exports had the characteristics of an economy undergoing the initial stages of industrial development. There were almost no brand products and little presence of high value added commodities. Exports were mostly labour intensive and composed of standard and basic products. However, these were also the products of sunset industries in industrialised countries that have become the object of intensive/vigorous anti-dumping claims. Anti-dumping investigations can win time and allow market share for those industries in developed countries to adjust as this normally will take longer with protection. US anti-dumping investigations against Chinese steel went on for a whole year and even though the final verdict was in China's favour, the damage was done. Some customers were lost and the stocks of the Chinese enterprises involved went into free fall on the stock market.

According to a Chinese Government source, 70 to 80 per cent of the total anti-dumping investigations against China are concentrated on textiles, chemicals, steel and mineral sectors, all of which are labour intensive and sectors characterised with low value added. Most of these industries are the sunset industries in developed countries that are at the same time the mainstay industries for countries undergoing the first stages of industrialisation. In the past three years, chemicals and metals still ranked foremost for anti-dumping investigations. Messerlin (2002) found that anti-dumping measures in metals, chemicals, machinery and electrical equipment, textiles and clothing, and plastics accounted for 75 per cent of the total number of measures. He also noticed that these products are characterised by a high proportion of relatively standard production and oligopolistic structures. He suspects that complaining firms use anti-dumping as an instrument to segment the market and squeeze out new rivals.

Ironically, although China has been treated as a non-market economy by some of its trading partners, the diminishing role of Government in production planning and the foreign trade has also led to duplicate investments and overcapacity. The Government is no longer directly involved in foreign trade although it continues to monitor its operations at an arms' length. For most export products, the Government's present function is to maintain a registry system. Manufacturers' associations have not acquired the capacity to influence production activities.

An increasing number of Chinese firms in the export sector are operating in a market environment where the purchase of inputs and the raising of finance are founded on commercial principles. Exporting enterprises however have yet to learn to operate more systematically—i.e., by conducting feasibility studies and business planning. Herd behaviour is prevalent; once a producer enters a major market, many others follow. In the process, not much attention has been paid to the overall volume and value increase in the export market. These huge increases do easily trigger anti-dumping petitions. Thus, there is still a lot to learn for the Government to perfect its use of fiscal, financial, legal and administrative measures that are allowed by WTO rules in order to guide the economy maintain a rational and balanced increased rate of fixed asset investments and so secure a stable and sustained development of the foreign trade sector.

Many exporting companies lack a good understanding of WTO Rules of Origin. As a result, the 'Made in China' label was placed on exports, which were, in fact, not really up to the threshold set by the Rules of Origin. This consequently has artificially boosted the actual volume of Chinese exports. With this working environment, the education of exporters and the enforcement of such rules should in principle form part of the Government's responsibilities.

In addition, the majority of enterprises resort to price competition for market entry and market expansion in both domestic and international markets. Product upgrading and differentiation is yet to be utilised as a tool to capture and maintain market share. A significant part of Chinese exports is still concentrated in such anti-dumping intensive products as textiles, clothing, footwear and travel items. One important reason for this phenomenon is that most of these products have low market entry cost. As product upgrading requires research and development and the recovery of this kind of sunk cost will take time, companies tend to avoid this type of strategic investment. Instead, there is a tendency for domestic entrepreneurs to rush to produce the same products at about the same time, thereafter creating a highly competitive situation. More often than not, exports are priced at extremely low levels with razor thin profits. Some anti-dumping charges may have been well substantiated because intense price competition in China may push enterprises into periods of selling at a loss.

China's heavy concentration of exports destinations as well as its dramatic expansion of trade is closely related with the rising importance of processing trade. Unlike Japan and the Republic of

Korea, which emphasised the development of their national brands and their own national giants with horizontal and vertical production specialisation, i.e., with the entire production process undertaken within their countries, China's trade expansion has relied heavily on processing trade.

From 1979 to the end of 2003, processing trade grew 243-fold (China Daily, 2004). Since 1995 processing trade has been the most important mode of foreign trade in China. Presently around 50 per cent of China's exports are processed (Figure 7.4). While there is a deficit under normal trade, China's total trade surplus mainly comes from processing trade—processing of imported materials accounts for three quarters of this trade while the remainder is taken up by the processing of material provided by foreign importers of the eventual finished products.

Figure 7.4

Trend of Processing Trade by China

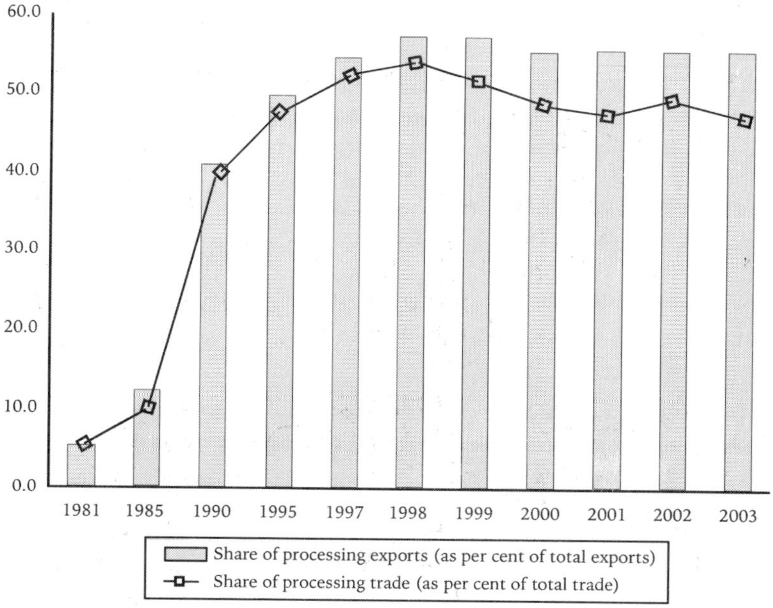

Source : General Administration of Customs of China.

Processing trade was started by companies in Asian NIEs. Most of them were small-scale companies, which concentrated on labour-intensive goods, including goods that were anti-dumping intensive and from sunset sectors. This reflects the famous flying geese model of development with early industrialisers moving up the production ladder and passing on the traditional sectors to the latecomers. While upgrading their exports from standard basic products into more differentiated products, Hong Kong (China), Japan, Singapore, the Republic of Korea, and Taiwan Province of China transferred some of their traditional and anti-dumping intensive operations into China where labour and infrastructure costs were relatively cheap. This transfer has provided China with the badly needed job opportunities and has also extended product life cycles and profit margins by cutting production costs. This arrangement represents a win-win situation for both China and NIEs. One drawback however is that it is prone to trade disputes.

Around the mid-1990s, the processing trade in China entered into a different stage. This has had a profound change on its export compositions but seemed to further accentuate the imbalance in export destinations. Processing trade, which was formerly exclusively labour-intensive, became rather capital-intensive as overseas businesses invested heavily in manufacturing of high-tech products such as computer hardware, chemicals and auto parts. Machinery and electronic products now contribute to over half of China's overall exports and about 70 per cent of the entire processing trade volume. This does not mean China's technological level in these products has reached the competitive levels of developed countries. It is rather that the Chinese firms are mainly responsible for the final stages of the production, a division of labour characterised by lower-wage countries for lower-end production, whereas higher-end activities are focused on countries where costs are higher.

According to the Ministry of Commerce, in 2003 around 80 per cent of the processing trade was financed by overseas investors (China Daily, 2004). However, the import contents of these exports are quite high and mostly come from Asian countries. The production of these firms in China, however, relies on imports of machineries to set up the operation, and then imports parts and components for processing and final assembly. While Chinese workers earn a tiny share of the total value of the products in the form of wages, multinational firms are making handsome profits out of these activities. A major source of imports for assembling and re-exporting are from Asian economies. This type of 'vertical specialisation' in the production process in the Asian region has resulted in China acquiring an increasingly important role in the final assembly stages of a broad range of export commodities. It has also intensified the heavy reliance on United States and European Union markets—the traditional export destinations for Asian exports.

Trade volume between China and the United States accounted for 5.4 per cent of China's GDP in 1997, but rose to 8.95 per cent in 2003. China is the source for the increasing share of goods exported to United States markets. These same goods were those previously produced by Japan, Taiwan Province of China, Singapore, the Republic of Korea and Hong Kong (China). As a result, China has been running big trade deficits with some Asian economies at the same time that it was experiencing a growing surplus with the United States. Some economists call this trade pattern as the "relocation of deficits". According to Chan (2003):

> The effect of 'relocation of deficits' can best be illustrated by the US trade deficits in electronic products, which increased from US$50.4 billion in 1998 to US$88.8 billion in 2002. This group of products is also important because the US deficit in these products with China came up to as much as US$31.4 billion in 2002, more than one-third of the Sino-US total trade deficit registered in US official figures.... Apparently, US deficits in electronics with China grew by US$17.0 billion during 1998-2002. However, US deficits with Japan decreased by US$7.1 billion and those with Taiwan fell by US$1.5 billion. The 'relocation of deficits' thus constituted more than a half of the increase in Sino-US trade imbalance in electronic products.

As a result, the increased trade surplus has been far from being proportionate to the increase of the trade volume. The size of current account balance has been declining over the last few years up to 2002. Proportionately, in 2002, the weight of the current account surplus over the entire balance of payments has reduced by close to 40 per cent in comparison with the situation in 2000.

China's WTO accession protocol states that the country may be treated, on a case-by-case basis, as a non-market economy (NME) for anti-dumping purposes until 2016. The issue of whether or not it is fair to regard China as a NME is not the subject of this chapter. However, it needs to be said that being categorised as an NME greatly increases the possibility of a positive dumping ruling and places China at a disadvantage. With this clause in China's accession protocol, the burden to prove 'less than normal value' and 'material injury' would be much lighter. As a matter of fact it has also given rise to abuse as production costs can be calculated according to those that are from a surrogate country. Since the surrogate country had not been chosen by the Chinese, it has often transpired that the countries that were chosen were places where material and labour costs were much higher than in China, which definitely do not lay the foundation for a fair assessment in anti-dumping cases. There are opportunities to manipulate data, which in greater likelihood result in a positive ruling of a case. In addition, an assessment of this kind of data could also result in much higher dumping margins, and lead to higher punitive anti-dumping duties. There is also a domino effect as the whole process can be executed relatively easily and the chances of success are high, this in turn leads to a higher level of anti-dumping incidences.

The lack of legal capacity on the part of Chinese enterprises to respond to anti-dumping investigations abroad is also a factor contributing to the frequency of final anti-dumping measures against Chinese exports. In the past, most of the Chinese exporters were unaware of the anti-dumping process. So when their products were accused of being dumped, their first response was bewilderment and panic. When they learnt of the cost of anti-dumping litigations, they invariably pulled out. As a result, no-response and absentee rulings were quite common, which means affirmative injury ruling was almost a certainty. The lack of qualified staff with good knowledge of the language of the country bringing the case and anti-dumping practice also prevented Chinese enterprises from defending their interests. In this situation the vulnerability of Chinese farmers is unparalleled because most of them are still not aware about dumping and anti-dumping practices. In addition, China had never had any producer/manufacturers' associations before, nor did it have powerful and effective interest groups, which can be found in industrialised countries. When each enterprise fought its own battle, their strength definitely could not match their foreign counterparts.

'Echoing' anti-dumping investigations happen very often to China (Maur, 1998). When a complaint was filed in one country, producers in other countries quickly followed suit. The absence of an immediate response from China after an anti-dumping petition has been filed and the ease with which a positive ruling could be obtained encourages competitors to free ride. This is not only because of fear of trade diversion; it is also a strategic response in order to reduce future competition by eliminating a rival.

The United States and European Union have for many years topped the list of those submitting anti-dumping cases against China. However, as China's exports are highly concentrated in these markets, China does not have much leverage against anti-dumping investigations originating in these markets. Chinese retaliation against anti-dumping activities has been very measured for fear of upsetting major importers, and has thus never constituted a strategic threat to them. The absence of built-in counter-force and credible threat to these markets has placed China at the receiving end of trade restrictive measures. However, with the increase in recent years of both FDI inflows and exports from the United States into China, the situation has, to some degree, been mitigated. China has now even filed anti-dumping cases against the United States.

Prusa (2002: 9) has pointed out that countries generally have significant discretion in the use of anti-dumping law because of the way in which anti-dumping statutes are drafted. Thus, countries and individual industries within countries have learned that they can use the laws to their advantage in a several ways. So if politically and strategically China-bashing during a United States election year is to their advantage, there would be more anti-dumping activities against China. It has been a routine practice to increase trade frictions between the United States and China every election year.

Even though the total number of anti-dumping investigations initiated worldwide has decreased over the past two years, some large developing countries, including China, have increased their use of anti-dumping mechanism. China is also a target of anti-dumping investigations from developing countries. Since 2002, India has replaced the United States as the number one country in launching anti-dumping investigations against Chinese exports. On average, anti-dumping duties from developing countries are higher than those imposed by industrial countries. One example is Mexico, which levied punitive tariffs on Chinese footwear as high as 1,105 per cent.

It needs to be pointed out there is a fundamental difference between anti-dumping activities between those initiated by the developing countries and developed countries. Developing countries have little capacity to engage in FDI activities to jump anti-dumping.

Nor do these countries have latitude to collude with MNEs to squeeze out new rivals. These countries' major concern is to protect domestic producers since it is not possible to rely on tariff protection *vis-à-vis* widespread trade liberalisation. Developing countries neither have the financial capacity to provide domestic support or subsidies to the same degree as the developed countries.

There are two important reasons behind the increasing anti-dumping investigations from developing countries against Chinese exports. Firstly, developing countries, with the support of their governments, become more aware of anti-dumping procedures. Secondly, being at the same stage of development and with exports coming from similar traditional sectors increases the factor that developing countries may be at loggerheads with one another not only in some international but also in domestic markets. Thirdly, the blatant double standard of developed countries in dumping heavily subsidised agricultural products into developing countries and beyond, and their abuse of anti-dumping have made developing countries think they too have to play the same game.

Conclusion

There have been a number of criticisms about the methodology used to determine dumping, particularly with regard to its opaqueness and the resulting ease of manipulation. For many years, developed countries have been heavy users of anti-dumping activities to protect their sunset industries, and their MNEs have used anti-dumping as a weapon to strengthen monopoly rather than to enhance a 'level playing field'. The inherent weakness and loopholes of anti-dumping laws are among the reasons why China is a target of anti-dumping activities, as it is a new and relatively efficient new rival in the world market. The WTO members are currently negotiating within the Negotiation Group on Rules to further clarify and improve the Agreement on Anti-dumping. According to the Doha Ministerial Declaration which was adopted on 14 November 2001, the ongoing negotiation is "aimed at clarifying and improving disciplines" instead of changing the basic concepts and principles, which means anti-dumping activities will continue to have an important impact on international trade.

The present stage of development and development model of the People's Republic of China has determined that in addition to expanding its domestic consumption, trade expansion is as essential for its economic growth. Its trade structure, with the increasing importance of processing trade, may provide the badly needed job opportunities. This may also allow for the relocation of some sunset industrial sectors, and consolidate and expand the existing heavy concentration of export destinations. Although China's export composition has undergone drastic changes, its role as an assembler and final stage producer does place it at a disadvantage when it comes to anti-dumping activities. In the long run, however, it is necessary for China to shift its export products away from anti-dumping-intensive sectors by upgrading export products from standard products into highly differentiated products. The development of China's own brand of products, and undertaking a horizontal production for some important dynamic products can also minimise exposure to foreign anti-dumping charges against Chinese exports and thereby reduce financial losses. In view of the cost of anti-dumping to the economy, it is now time for China to put into place a screening mechanism as permitted by the WTO accession conditions before engaging itself in new processing trade deals.

The extensive safeguard provisions that are included in China's WTO accession commitments could constrain China's export growth. Moreover, intensified anti-dumping activities against Chinese exports will not only be detrimental to China's trade balance; it will also hurt the world. China's track record for trade and economic performance has shown that the benefits of its trade expansion have been distributed much more broadly than the same done under some earlier NIEs. This is because in a globalising world, China's exports rely heavily on foreign capital, imports of primary, intermediary and capital goods.

References

Chan, Thomas M.H. (2003). "It's Wrong to Blame China for US Trade Deficit", *China Daily*, 29 December.

China Daily (2003). "Furniture Makers to Fight Dumping Charges", (Hong Kong edition), 6 November.

———. (2004). "Processing Trade to Get a Boost", 15 January.

Farrell, D., S. Ghai and T. Shavers (2005). "A Silver Lining in the US Trade Deficit", *The McKinsey Quarterly*, March 2005, various pages.

Frenkel, S. (2001). "Globalization, Athletic Footwear Commodity Chains and Employment Relations in China", *Organization Studies*, 22(4). ABI.INFORM Global.

Gereffi, G., F. Palpacuer and A. Parisotto (1999). *Global Production and Local Jobs,* International Labour Office, Geneva, Switzerland.

Harney, A. (2004). "Chinese Factories Roll Out More Perks to Woo Workers", *Financial Times,* 19 March.

Maur, J.C. (1998). "Echoing Anti-dumping Cases, Regulatory Competitors, imitation and cascading protection", Groupe d'Economie Mondiale & Institute d'Etudes Politiques de Paris.

McCaughrin, R. (2004). "Dispelling Trade Myths, Global Economic Forum", Morgan Stanley, 5 April, in *http://www.morganstanley.com/GEFdata/digests/20040405-mon.html#anchor1.*

Messerlin, P.A. (2002). "China in the WTO: Anti-dumping and Safeguards", *American Economic Review* 2602.

Miranda, J., R. Torres and M. Ruid (1998). "The International Use of Anti-dumping: 1987–1997", *Journal of World Trade,* 32(5):5–71.

Nolan, P. and Jin Zhang (2002). "The Challenge of Globalization for Large Chinese Firms", *UNCTAD Discussion Papers,* No. 162, July, Geneva, United Nations Conference on Trade and Development.

People's Daily, (2003). "Frequent Anti-dumping Bangs, Perfecting Early Warning System is a Must", 24 June.

Pierce, R.J. Jr. (1999). "Anti-dumping Law as Means of Facilitating Cartelization", *Public Law and Legal Theory Working Paper* 002, George Washington University Law School.

Prusa, T.J. and S. Skeath (2002). Retaliation as an Explanation for the Proliferation of Anti-dumping.

Rumbaugh, T. and N. Blancherm (2004). "China: International Trade and WTO Accession", *IMF Working Paper,* WP/04/36. Washington, DC, International Monetary Fund.

United States, International Trade Administration, Department of Commerce, Fact Sheet.

Vandenbussche, H., R. Veugelers and R. Belderbos (1999). "Undertakings and Anti-dumping Jumping FDI in Europe".

WTO (2004). World Trade Organization Press Releases, various issues.

Yan, Dai (2004). "Final Ruling Fails to Surprise", *China Daily,* 20 April.

Zanardi, M. (2004). "Anti-dumping: What are the Numbers to Discuss at Doha?" *World Economy,* 27(3), pp. 403-433.

8

Misuse of Anti-Dumping Provisions: What do the WTO Disputes Reveal?

DEBASHIS CHAKRABORTY[1]

Introduction

WTO-incompatibility of Anti-Dumping measures (henceforth ADM) of various countries is a much-debated issue in the trade policy literature. The purpose of the WTO Agreement on Anti-Dumping (henceforth ADA) is to ensure the use of Anti-Dumping Duties (henceforth ADD) only as a contingency measure among member countries, and not as a protectionist mechanism. Although, the industrial tariff level has significantly declined in a number of WTO members, the misuse of AD provisions have significantly lowered the extent of realised market access. It is observed that the WTO agreement has failed to limit the misuse of various provisions under this agreement and over the last decade it has evolved as a major trade-distorting mechanism, benefiting domestic industries of the initiators.[2] The improper usage of ADA has often highlighted the need to reform the WTO agreement (Lindsey and Ikenson, 2002; Raju, 2004). It has been noted from time to time that there exist several loopholes in the provision, through which a country can practice protectionist measures (Banik, 1998; Debroy and Banik, 2000; Aggarwal, 2004). It is observed that among the 14 cases lodged at WTO DSB up to 30th September 2006, 6 cases involve AD (DS 346—ADM on oil country tubular goods from Argentina in US; DS 345—Customs Bond Directive for merchandise subject to ADM from India in US; DS 344—Final ADM on Stainless Steel from Mexico in US; DS 343—ADM on Shrimp export from Thailand in US; DS 338—provisional ADM on Grain Corn export from US by Canada; DS 337—ADM on Farmed Salmon export from Norway by EC).

1. The views expressed in this chapter are personal.
2. "The anti-dumping are simply a popular means by which domestic firms can stifle foreign competition under the pretence of 'fair trade'," Irwin (2002), p. 127.

The 'globalisation' of anti-dumping measures being a major problem in the trade arena, there is an urgent need to respond to it. While in the earlier period the usage of this provision was not so frequent among the developing countries, the trend has changed drastically during the recent years, as the WTO Annual Report (2003: 10-11) notes:

> The increasing use of contingency measures, particularly anti-dumping actions, is also a key area of interest to Members. Although the upward trend was somewhat reversed in 2001, when the number of new anti-dumping measures in force fell to 159 from 235 in the previous year, this is still considerably greater than the numbers imposed in 1995, 1996 and 1997. More Members, including developing countries, are resorting to them increasingly. The rising trend in the use of such measures prompted Members to place the matter on the DDA.

The effectiveness and rationale of anti-dumping procedure in order to curb cheaper import, marketed at a supposedly 'unfair' price, is questionable. It has been shown in the subsequent analysis that while initiating the investigations and imposing final duties, the 'home government' often does not conform to the WTO norms. In a significant number of cases, the imposition of ADD has been proved WTO-incompatible (Table 8.1). There is no doubt about the fact that the dumping procedure ends up significantly hurting the interest of the domestic consumers. In this scenario, a serious debate should follow on urgent modification, and in the extreme case, the justification behind continuation of ADA under the wings of WTO.

The chapter is organised along the following lines. First, we briefly discuss the violation of ADA articles in WTO cases lodged at DSB and the major sub-articles under ADA, which have been misused frequently. The relevant information for the analysis is obtained from the recent DSB update (WTO, 2005). Then we look into the anti-dumping cases involving India, and the changing perspective of the country in this issue. Finally, on the basis of the observations, some future concerns are noted.

A Global Scenario

First we focus on the cases lodged at the DSB, and by analysing the alleged violations made in the submissions by the appellant; an attempt is made to identify the extent of misuse of various articles of

ADA. The article-level analysis is summarised in Figure 8.1. It is observed that maximum number of disputes at WTO is lodged questioning the imposition of Article 5 (concerning initiation procedures and subsequent investigation) and Article 2 (determination of dumping); followed by Article 3 (determination of injury to domestic industry) and Article 6 (concerning evidence) respectively. The high incidence of DSB cases on these categories speaks out the potential of mishandling of anti-dumping cases on these grounds, which actually covers almost the entire procedure. Indeed, the determination of 'dumping' and estimating the 'injury' has been a major bone of contention. Other ADA provisions allegedly misused are Article 1 (conformity of applied procedures with the ADA), Article 12 (public notification of the procedures and explanation of the determinations), Article 18 (procedures relating to final provisions) and Annex II (determination on the basis of best information available when collecting direct evidence is a problem). It has been alleged by affected countries at times that the notification procedure, a much-needed measure for ensuring transparency, is seldom properly followed. Furthermore, the clause 'best available information' is subject to various interpretations, and could be utilised

Figure 8.1

Alleged Violation of WTO Anti-Dumping Agreement—Article-wise

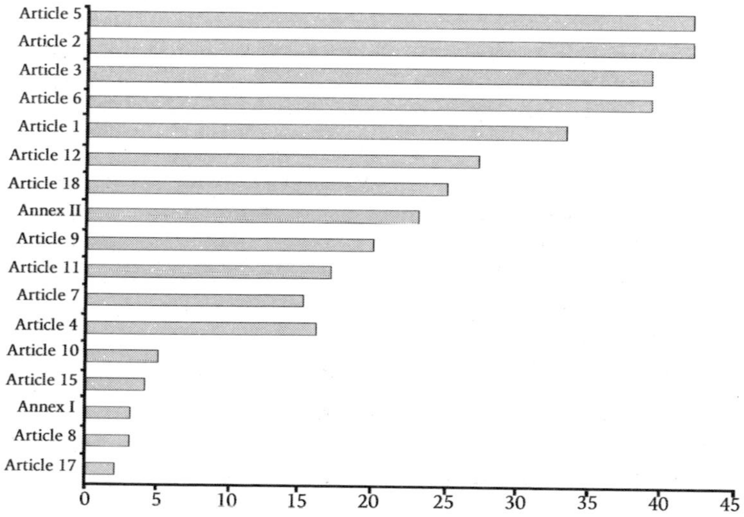

by any country to tilt the result of the investigation in its favour. Further down the list, alleged violation takes place on the ground of Article 9 (imposition and collection of ADD), Article 11 (duration and review of ADD and price undertakings), Article 7 (provisional measures) and Article 4 (definition of domestic industry). While the affected exporters have claimed at various occasions that the imposition of provisional measures as well as the duration and review of ADD often do not reflect the reality, the very basis of the initiation, i.e., harm to a significant section of 'industry' (Article 4), has been challenged at times. Among other alleged violations, Article 15 (special regard to developing countries), Annex I (procedures regarding on the spot investigations) and Article 8 (price undertakings) deserves mentioning. In short, the fact that only a handful of less important articles in ADA did not attract any alleged violation over the last 10 years, clearly shows the misuse of the provisions at large and raises serious questions about the very procedure.

We further extend the analysis by focusing on the measures ruled WTO-incompatible by the DSB (both panel and appellate bodies). An article is dropped from the analysis if it is ruled WTO-incompatible by the panel, but reversed by the appellate body. The findings are illustrated with the help of Figure 8.2. The observations are briefly summarised in the following:

- First, Article 2.4 ('fair comparison' between export price and normal value) is declared WTO-incompatible maximum number of times, followed by Article 3.4 (consideration of 'all relevant economic factors' for determination of dumping) and Article 6.8 (final determination on the basis of 'available facts'). These three clauses, taken together, shows that the determination of the dumping margin and the investigation procedure is often not in line with the obligation of members under WTO. Similarly, violations of Annex II (determination on the basis of best information available when collecting direct evidence is a problem) and Article 3.5 (demonstration of causal relationship between dumped import and injury) are also quite high, as attested by the DSB, five times. Especially, non-market economies have suffered most from this provision.
- Second, the determination related concerns, i.e., Article 3.1 (examination of the impact of dumped imports on prices of domestic 'like products' and their producers), Article 3.2

(investigation on significant increase in dumped imports and price undercutting) and Article 18.4 (adoption of 'all necessary steps' to conform with ADA) have been declared WTO-incompatible four times each. This shows that the investigations initiated are not often backed by necessary background works by the home country, where only protectionist mindset is to be blamed. In other words, the inclination towards imposition of ADD has been too evident.

- Third, Article 5.8 (immediate termination of investigations in the absence of sufficient evidence), Article 12.1 (public notification of sufficient evidence to reach the interested parties), Article 18.1 (imposition of no specific action in disagreement with GATT 1994) and Article 2.2 (procedure for collecting cost and profit data) are ruled WTO-incompatible three times each. Absence of WTO-compatibility in terms of all the four provisions attests the lack of enthusiasm among the violators to conform to ADA, and a willingness to protect the domestic industry.
- A number of provisions have been declared WTO-incompatible twice. These provisions include Article 4.1 (definition of domestic producers), Article 5.3 (examination of the accuracy and adequacy of the evidence provided), Article 6.2 (providing full opportunity to all interested parties to defend their interests throughout the investigation), Article 6.4 (timely opportunities for all interested parties to see all information), Article 6.9 (full opportunity to all interested parties to defend their interests before final determination), Article 11.2 (reviewing of the need for continuing the duty after the lapse of 'reasonable period of time'), Article 3.7 (determination of threat on the basis of facts, and not merely on allegation, conjecture or remote possibility) and Article 12.2 (detailed notification of the findings) and others. The provisions violated once include, Article 5.2 (evidence of dumping, injury and their causal link in the written application), Article 10.4 (imposition of definitive ADD only after determination of threat).
- Finally, the potential of practicing WTO-incompatibility under various articles of ADA, as reflected from the DSB rulings, are summarised in Figure 8.3. It is observed that the actions under Article 3 (determination of injury to domestic industry–25%),

Figure 8.2

Actual Violations of WTO Anti-Dumping Agreement—DSB Rulings

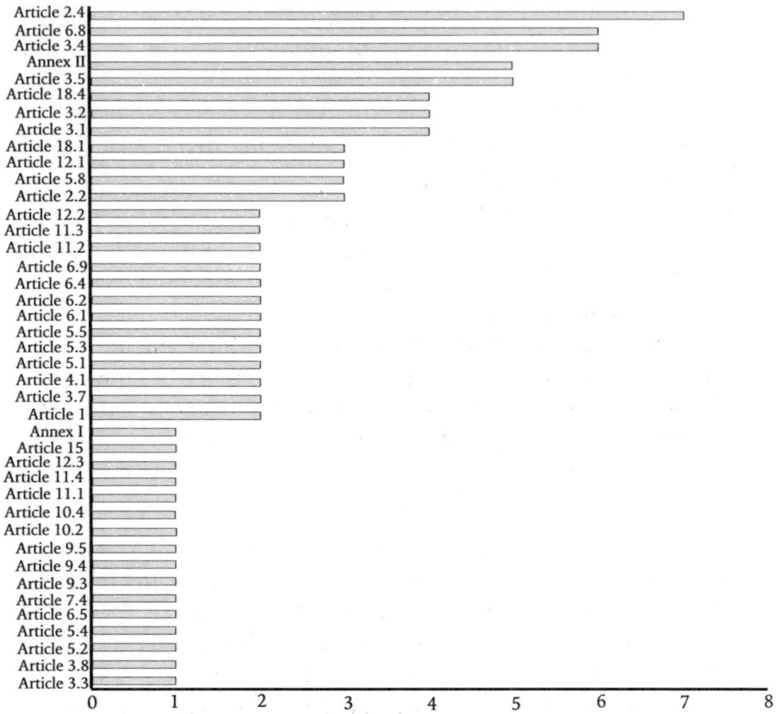

Article 6 (the procedures concerning evidence–18%), Article 5 (relating to initiation procedures and subsequent investigation–11%) and Article 2 (determination of dumping–10%) have been proved WTO-incompatible most frequently. In short, this observation puts a question mark on the entire process of dumping determination mechanism and the role of domestic industry behind it.

To have an overall assessment of the trends in ADA cases, we present the outcome of the complaints lodged at DSB over 1996-2004 under seven different categories, following the framework used by Chakraborty and Chaisse (2005). In the first two columns, we present 'win' and 'loss' in a particular case. We define 'win' by a complainant if it wins at the panel level, even if the appellate body reverses certain legal interpretations of the verdict later, since the existence of a WTO-

Figure 8.3

Distribution of Violations of Anti-Dumping Agreement as per DSB Ruling

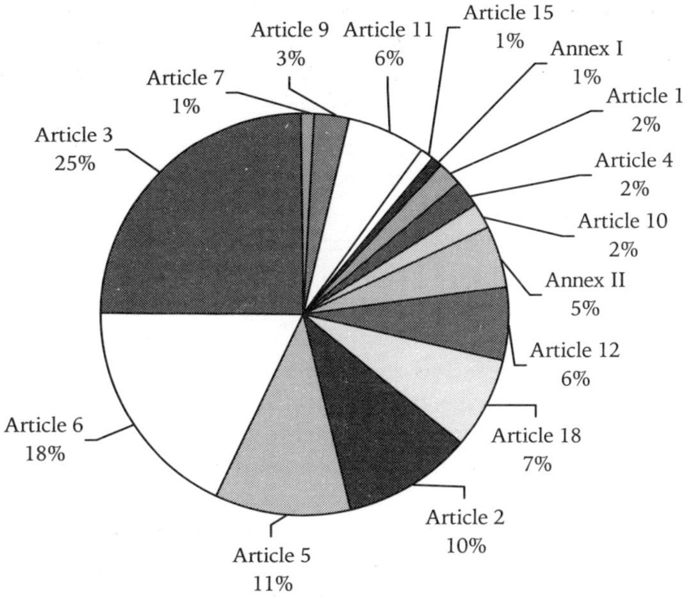

incompatible policy has been established. However, rejection of the claims, both at panel and appellate body level, is termed as 'loss'. In the third column, under the head 'continuing', we have clubbed three options—cases with ongoing review, cases currently with the appellate body and cases where verdict is expected within a specified time. The fourth column deals with the joint request of the parties to DSB for suspension of proceeding after the panel has been formed, which shows that either of the two sides is willing to negotiate on the alleged measures in force. Fifth, we note the cases where no panel had been formed, which show mutual discussion, probably leading the respondent to guarantee the desired market access for the complainant to resolve the dispute. Two other possibilities cannot be ruled out in this case. First, (if a developed country) the complaint might have been raised for harassing the respondent as a trade policy instrument, and second, (if a developing country) the complainant might have lacked the necessary technical expertise to support his claim, and decided to opt out before formation of the panel. Sixth, we note the cases where a mutually agreeable solution has been notified to the DSB. In the final column the cases where the alleged measure was promptly discontinued after the initial notification at DSB are placed. We feel that this option is quite important. On one hand, this indicates the existence of WTO-incompatible measures in force, and highlights the effectiveness of the dispute settlement mechanism on the other as a credible threat mechanism.

The results of the analysis are summarised in Table 8.1. Apart from looking at the overall scenario, we also focus on the US, which is the largest violator of the provision (in terms of cases lodged against it). From the overall scenario reported in the upper panel, we see that every third case lodged at the DSB has represented a valid concern, i.e., the existence of WTO-incompatibility of the provision in question has been proved. Only in two occasions, the complaints have been defeated. There has been no request to suspend the panel proceeding on the issue of dumping till date, and on one occasion amicable settlement has been notified to the WTO. In a large number of cases (25), no panel has been formed. Finally, on three occasions, the respondent has removed the alleged WTO-incompatible measure (DS 23—involving Venezuela as respondent, DS 89— involving the US as respondent and DS 313—involving the EC as respondent) after initial request for consultation was made to the DSB.

The analysis involving the US as respondent has been reported in the lower panel of Table 8.1. It is observed that almost 50 per cent of the total number of cases relating to ADA has been lodged against it. Since the analysis is done on the basis of complaints, column A represents the cases, where the US practices has been defeated. Column B on the other hand represents the scenario when the US policies in question were ruled WTO-consistent by the WTO. Two points deserve particular mention. First, it is observed that US accounts for more than 50 per cent of the cases where the policies of the importing country have been ruled WTO-incompatible. Second, only the US has been able to twice win a case as respondent (DS 221 —involving Canada as appellant, DS 244—involving Japan as appellant).

The analysis carried so far indicates gross violation of the ADA procedures and consequent worsening of consumer welfare in the importing country. It also highlights the efficiency of the WTO dispute

Table 8.1

*Analysis of DSB Complaints**

Overall Analysis of Anti-Dumping Cases								
Year	*A*	*B*	*C*	*D*	*E*	*F*	*G*	*Total*
1996	1	0	0	0	1	1	1	4
1997	1	0	0	0	1	0	1	3
1998	4	0	0	0	1	0	0	5
1999	4	0	0	0	4	0	0	8
2000	3	0	0	0	4	0	0	7
2001	4	1	0	0	4	0	0	9
2002	2	1	0	0	3	0	0	6
2003	0	0	4	0	2	0	0	6
2004	0	0	2	0	5	0	1	8
Total	**19**	**2**	**6**	**0**	**25**	**1**	**3**	**56**
Countries Complaining against United States' Anti-Dumping Policies								
Year	*A*	*B*	*C*	*D*	*E*	*F*	*G*	*Total*
1996	0	0	0	0	1	1	0	2
1997	1	0	0	0	0	0	1	2
1998	1	0	0	0	0	0	0	1
1999	3	0	0	0	0	0	0	3
2000	1	0	0	0	0	0	0	1
2001	2	1	0	0	2	0	0	5
2002	2	1	0	0	2	0	0	5
2003	0	0	3	0	0	0	0	3
2004	0	0	1	0	3	0	0	4
Total	**10**	**2**	**4**	**0**	**8**	**1**	**1**	**26**

Source : Constructed from Dispute Settlement Updates, WTO (2005).

Notes :

* A – Win for appellant B – Loss for respondent
C – Continuing/Result expected soon D – Request to suspend panel proceeding
E – Panel not formed F – Amicably settled
G – Discontinuation of the alleged measure by the respondent

settlement procedure, despite certain limitations, in no uncertain terms. Given this trend, we focus on the anti-dumping cases involving India (both as an appellant as well as respondent) in the following.

Anti-Dumping Disputes Involving India: A Review of Issues

Before going into the discussion of anti-dumping cases involving India, a comparative analysis of the two trade policy review reports on India will not be irrelevant here. While the first review (1998) has been critical of India on various accounts like tariff reform, import restriction procedures, absence of full compliance with TRIPS, lack of liberalisation of domestic service sectors etc., the last review (2002) praised the reform measures already undertaken during the inter-survey years.[3] The concerns raised over India's unfinished reform agenda in the WTO (2002) review were not too many in number, but it categorically identified the increasing trend in anti-dumping investigations as one of the major problem areas:

> India has become one of the major users of anti-dumping measures, with some 250 cases initiated since 1995... Moreover, the number of anti-dumping measures in force has risen steadily, especially since 1997, from 19 notified measures in force, to 131 in 2001 (Chart III.3). The majority of the initiations have been for chemical and related products (47.2%); a large number of actions have been initiated against imports from the European Union (19.2%) and China (18.8%).

In general, the increasing usage of anti-dumping procedures by India has caught the attention of the international community. The WTO Annual Report (2004: 47) noted, "Of the 1323 measures in force reported, 21 per cent were maintained by the United States, 16 per cent by India, 15 per cent by the European Communities, 7 per cent each by South Africa and Canada, and 6 per cent by Argentina. Other members reporting measures in force each accounted for 5 per cent or less of the total." Since the publication of the 2002 review, India has faced three cases at the DSB as respondent, all of which have been filed on the working of the anti-dumping procedures. In particular, the recent request by EC for consultation on imposition of anti-dumping measures in India on 27 commodities (DS 304)[4], followed by complaints of Bangladesh (DS 306) and Taiwan (DS 318) shows the

---

3. The non-notification of a single case against India at DSB for a long time (1999–2002) signifies the increasing WTO-compatibility of India's domestic regulations. Chakraborty and Chaisse (2005).

4. The details about the consultation are outlined in WTO Document WT/DS304/1 (Dated 11 December 2003).

seriousness of the claims.[5] The results of these three cases will have profound implication for all future cases against India in this area. The US and China has also raised concerns over the frequent initiations of anti-dumping investigations in India:

> India's implementation of its anti-dumping regime has raised concerns in key areas such as transparency and due process. India continued to apply aggressively its anti-dumping law over the past year. According to WTO statistics, India initiated 13 (third highest among all WTO members) anti-dumping cases in 2005. In fact, from the second half of 2004 through the first half of 2005, which is the most recent 12-month period for which WTO statistics are available, India imposed 30 final anti-dumping measures, more than any other WTO Member, and ranked second in the number of initiations (USTR 2006, p. 313).

However, as seen from the excerpt from the annual report (2003-2004) of the Directorate General of Anti-Dumping and Allied Duties provided below, India claims that its procedures are in line with the relevant WTO provisions, although the three complaints testifies otherwise.

> The national legislation in respect of anti-dumping was put in place when the Customs Tariff (Identification, Assessment and Collection of duty or Additional duty on Dumped Articles and for Determination of Injury) Rules, 1985 were notified. Sections 9, 9A, 9AA, 9B and 9C of the Custom Tariff Act, 1975 as amended in July 1995 and the Customs Tariff (Identification, Assessment and Collection of Anti Dumping Duty on Dumped Articles and for Determination of Injury) Rules,1995 as amended (in July 1999 vide Notification No.44/1999; in May 2001 vide notification No.28/2001, in January 2002 vide Notification No.1/2002 of 4th January 2002 and in November 2003 vide Notification No. 101/2003-customs(Non-Tariff) dated 10.11.2003) and Customs Tariff (Identification, Assessment and Collection of Countervailing Duty on Subsidised Articles and for Determination of Injury) Rules, 1995 framed there under form the legal basis for anti-dumping and anti-subsidy investigations and for the levy of anti-dumping and countervailing duties. These laws are in conformity with the WTO's Agreement on implementation of Article VI of the GATT 1994, commonly known as Agreement on Anti-Dumping and Agreement on Subsidies & Countervailing Measures.

Table 8.2 notes the evolution of India in the global scenario of anti-dumping investigations, where the cases faced and imposed by three countries, EU, India and the US are compared. While in the initial years after WTO formation the initiations by India were not so

5. The case lodged by Bangladesh is particularly important owing to the fact that this is the first time a developing country and an Asian country has moved to DSB against it.

Table 8.2

Comparison of Anti-Dumping Initiations Involving EU, India and the US

Period	*India*		*EU**		*US*	
	A	*B*	*A*	*B*	*A*	*B*
1 January 1995–31 December 1995	5	3	33	21	13	6
1 January 1996–31 December 1996	20	10	23	35	21	21
1 January 1997–31 December 1997	13	7	41	59	16	15
1 January 1998–31 December 1998	33	12	21	42	22	15
1 January 1999–30 June 1999	40	6	32	20	28	7
1 July 1999–30 June 2000	27	11	49	32	29	10
1 July 2000–30 June 2001	37	-	29	-	77	-
1 July 2001–30 June 2002	76	12	23	39	58	11
1 July 2002–30 June 2003	67	12	15	32	29	12
1 July 2003–30 June 2004	37	14	18	19	42	23

Source : WTO Annual Reports (various issues).

A – Anti-dumping investigations initiated by the country;

B – Anti-dumping investigations initiated against the country.

Note *: The data includes the anti-dumping measures imposed on individual EU member states as well.

high, it increased steadily up to June 1999, but declined during the next period. However, the investigations increased from July 2000 onwards, and have surpassed the number of investigations initiated by the EU and the US during the last two periods noted. Furthermore, in Table 8.3, we summarise the last three cases lodged against India, all on the alleged violation of anti-dumping measures, in order to analyse the problems associated with the procedures followed. Since no panel report has been released on these cases till date, we look at the alleged violations as reported in the table. The alleged violations common in all three cases are on the ground of Article 1 (conformity of applied procedures with the ADA), Article 3.1 (examination of the impact of dumped imports on prices of domestic 'like products' and their producers), Article 3.2 (investigation on significant increase in dumped imports and price undercutting), Article 3.5 (demonstration of causal relationship between dumped import and injury), Article 6.8 (final determination on the basis of 'available facts'), Article 6.9 (full opportunity to all interested parties to defend their interests before final determination), Article 12.2 (detailed notification of the findings) and Annex II. Given the fact that many of these provisions have been

Table 8.3

India at the DSB on Anti-Dumping Issues as Respondent

Case No	*Complainant*	*Alleged Violation*	*WTO Ruling*
DS 318 (2004)	Separate Customs Territory of Taiwan, Penghu, Kinmen and Matsu	The provisional and definitive anti-dumping measures imposed by India on the seven chemical and related products are inconsistent with— • Article VI:1 and VI:2 of GATT 1994 • Articles 1, 2, 3.1, 3.2, 3.3, 3.4, 3.5, 3.7, 3.8, 4, 5, 6 (including Annex II), 7.4, 12.1 and 12.2 of the ADA	Consultation in progress.
DS 306 (2004)	Bangladesh	The Anti-Dumping measures are inconsistent with— • Articles I:1 and II:1; Article VI including Articles VI:1, VI:2 and VI:6(a) and Articles XXIII:1(a) and XXIII:1(b) of GATT 1994 • Articles 1, 2.1, 2.2, 2.4, 3.1, 3.2, 3.3, 3.4, 3.5, 3.7, 5.4, 5.8, 6.2, 6.4, 6.5, 6.8 (including para. 3 of Annex II), 6.9 and 12.2 of the Anti-Dumping Agreement.	Consultation in progress.
DS 304 (2003)	European Communities	The Anti-Dumping measures are inconsistent with— • Article VI:1 of GATT 1994 • Articles 1, 3.1, 3.2, 3.5, 6.6, 6.8 (including Annex II), 6.9 and 12.2 of the Anti-dumping Agreement.	Consultation in progress.

Source : Constructed from Dispute Settlement Updates, WTO (2005).

proved WTO-incompatible earlier in several disputes, we can argue that India is also sharing the global mindset.

In Table 8.4, the seven cases involving India as complainant over ADA violation has been summarised. The last case has been lodged in June 2006 against the US. In the second last case (DS 313—involving the EC), the measures at issue, violation of Articles 3.4, 3.5, 4.1 and 9.2 of the ADA, were withdrawn after India moved to the DSB, which could be termed as a success. On three occasions (DS 229—involving Brazil, DS 168—involving South Africa, DS 140—involving the EC), no panel has been formed although India alleged major violations in the working of the anti-dumping investigations in each case. On the remaining three occasions, the DSB bodies have ruled in India's favour. In DS 141 (involving EC) although the panel rejected several claims made by India, the measures applied by EC were ruled WTO-inconsistent on the ground of Article 2.4 ('fair comparison' between export price and normal value), Article 3.4 (consideration of 'all relevant economic factors' for determination of dumping) and Article 15 (developing country concerns). In DS 206 (involving the US), again despite getting most of the claims rejected, India was able to prove WTO-inconsistency of certain US policies. Finally, in DS 217 (involving US), the US procedures were ruled WTO-incompatible with respect to Article 5.4 (support to the application by domestic industry), Article 18.1 (imposition of no specific action in disagreement with GATT 1994) and Article 18.4 (adoption of 'all necessary steps' to conform with ADA) of the ADA. It is interesting to note that the violations faced by India in foreign markets (both developed and developing) and the alleged violations made by it at home are mostly different.

Apart from direct involvements, India has at times participated in the DSB process as an interested third party. We note India's participation in that capacity in Table 8.5. It is interesting to observe that in all the five cases mentioned in the table, the US has been the respondent. The interest in the cases involving the US probably originated from the fact that India fought two cases with the latter as respondent. However, it deserves mention that the results of the cases are quite diverse. While in two cases, the US policies were ruled WTO-incompatible (DS 136 and DS 162—involving the EC and Japan; DS 234—involving Canada and Mexico), in the other two the DSB ruled that the complaints failed to establish their claims (DS 221—involving Canada; DS 244—involving Japan).

Table 8.4

India at the DSB on Anti-Dumping Issues as Complainant

Case No.	Respondent	Alleged Violation	WTO Ruling
DS 345 (2006)	United States	The enhanced bond requirement under the Amended Bond Directive as applied to importers of the subject merchandise from India is inconsistent with – • Articles I, II, VI:2 (including Note 1 Ad Paragraphs 2 and 3 of Article VI), XI and XIII of the GATT • Articles 1, 7.1, 7.2, 7.4, 7.5, 9.2, 9.3, 9.3.1 and 18.1 of the ADA	No Panel formed.
DS 313 (2004)	European Communities	The EC measure is inconsistent with – • Articles 3, especially Articles 3.4 and 3.5; 4.1 and 9.2 of ADA	EC has agreed to terminate the measure at issue, and both parties have notified DSB of the mutual solution.
DS 229 (2001)	Brazil	The measures on Indian jute bags are inconsistent with – • Articles VI and X of GATT 1994 • Articles 1, 2, 3, 5, 6 (especially 6.6, 6.7, 6.8 and Annex II, 6.9, 6.10), 11, 12, 17.6(i), 18.3, 18.4 of the ADA • Article XVI of the WTO Agreement	No Panel formed.
DS 217 (2001)	United States	The amendment to the Tariff Act of 1930 signed on 28 October 2000 with the title of "Continued Dumping and Subsidy Offset Act of 2000" (known as "the Byrd Amendment") is inconsistent with – • Article 18.1 of the ADA in conjunction with Article VI:2 of the GATT and Article 1 of the ADA • Article 32.1 of the SCM Agreement, in conjunction with Article VI:3 of the GATT and Articles 4.10, 7.9 and 10 of the SCM Agreement • Article X(3)(a) of the GATT • Articles 5.4, 8 and 18.4 of the ADA • Articles 5, 11.4, 18 and 32.5 of the SCM Agreement	The Panel found that the CDSOA was inconsistent with – • Articles 5.4, 18.1 and 18.4 of the ADA • Articles 11.4, 32.1 and 32.5 of the SCM • Articles VI:2 and VI:3 of the GATT 1994 • Article XVI:4 of the WTO Agreement However it rejected the claim that CDSOA was inconsistent with – • Articles 8.3 and 15 of the ADA • Articles 4.10, 5 (b), 7.9 and 18.3 of the SCM • Article X:3 (a) of the GATT 1994 The Appellate Body upheld most of the major conclusions of the Panel.

Contd...

...Contd...

Case No.	*Respondent*	*Alleged Violation*	*WTO Ruling*
DS 206 (2000)	United States	The procedures under US anti-dumping and countervailing duty law were inconsistent with – • Articles VI and X of the GATT 1994 • Articles 1, 2, 3 (especially 3.3), 5 (especially 5.8), 6 (espe -cially 6.8), 12, 15, 18.4 and Annex II of the ADA • Articles 10, 11 (especially 11.9), 15 (especially 15.3), 22 and 27 (especially 27.10) of the SCM Agreement • Article XVI of the WTO Agreement	Although, the panel rejected India's claims relating to Articles 6.8, 15 and paragraphs 3, 5, and paragraph 7 of Annex II of the ADA, it concluded certain US practices to be WTO-incompatible.
DS 168 (1999)	South Africa	Anti-Dumping Duties on the Import of Certain Pharmaceutical Products from India are inconsistent with – • Articles 2, 3, 6(a) to (c) individually and in conjunction with 12, 12 and 15 of the ADA • Articles I and VI of GATT 1994	No Panel formed.
DS 141 (1998)	European Communities	The Anti-Dumping Duties on Imports of Cotton-Type Bed-Linen are inconsistent with – • Articles 2.2.2, 3.1, 3.2, 3.4, 3.5, 5.2, 5.3, 5.4, 5.8, 6, 12.2.2, and 15 of the ADA • Articles I and VI of the GATT 1994	Although, the panel rejected India's claims regarding Articles 2.2, 2.2.2, 3.1, 3.4, 3.5, 5.3, 5.4, and 12.2.2 of the ADA, it ruled that EC acted inconsistently with its obligations under Articles 2.4.2, 3.4, and 15 of the same Agreement. Later India won a case on the failure of the EC to bring its policy in line with its WTO obligation within the reasonable time.
DS 140 (1998)	European Communities	Anti-Dumping Investigations Regarding Unbleached Cotton Fabrics are inconsistent with – • Articles 2.2.1, 2.4.1, 2.4.2, 2.6, 3.3, 3.2, 3.4, 3.5, 4.1(I), 5.2, 5.3, 5.4, 5.5, 5.8, 6.10, 7.1(I), 7.4, 9.1, 9.2, 12.1, 12.2 and 15 of the ADA • Articles I and VI of GATT 1994	No Panel formed.

Source : Constructed from Dispute Settlement Updates, WTO (2005).

Table 8.5

Select Cases Involving India in DSB as Third Party

Case No.	*Complainant*	*Respondent*	*Dispute*	*Results*
DS 136 and DS 162	EC and Japan	United States	Anti-dumping Act of 1916	The Panel concluded that the US has acted inconsistently with Articles VI:1, VI:2 and XVI:4 of the GATT 1994 and Articles 1, 4.1, 5.1, 5.2, 5.4, 18.1 of the ADA. The Appellate Body upheld all of the findings and conclusions of the panel.
DS 221	Canada	United States	Section 129(c)(1) of the Uruguay Round Agreements Act	The Panel concluded that Canada had failed to establish that section 129(c)(1) of the Uruguay Round Agreements Act was inconsistent with Articles VI:2, VI:3 and VI:6(a) of the GATT 1994; Articles 1, 9.3, 11.1, 18.1 and 18.4 of the AD Agreement; Articles 10, 19.4, 21.1, 32.1 and 32.5 of the SCM Agreement; and Article XVI:4 of the WTO Agreement.
DS 234	Canada and Mexico	United States	Continued Dumping and Subsidy Offset Act of 2000	The Panel found that the CDSOA was inconsistent with Articles 5.4, 18.1 and 18.4 of the ADA, Articles 11.4, 32.1 and 32.5 of the SCM, Articles VI:2 and VI:3 of the GATT 1994 and Article XVI:4 of the WTO Agreement. However it rejected the claim that CDSOA was inconsistent with Articles 8.3 and 15 of the ADA, Articles 4.10, 5 (b) 7.9 and 18.3 of the SCM and Article X:3(a) of the GATT 1994. The Appellate Body upheld most of the major conclusions of the Panel.
DS 244	Japan	United States	Sunset review of anti-dumping duties on corrosion-resistant carbon steel flat products from Japan	The Panel rejected all of Japan's claims challenging various aspects of the US laws and regulations regarding the conduct of 'sunset' reviews of anti-dumping duties under US law. Although the Appellate Body reversed four of the Panel's legal findings, they concluded that the US had acted WTO-consistently.

Source : Constructed from Dispute Settlement Updates, WTO (2005).

Apart from the DSB cases, a number of Indian export items are subject to anti-dumping investigations in the export markets, and the issues are highlighted from time to time (ESCAP, 2000). Recently, the debate over shrimps with US has come to forefront. Last year, US International Trade Commission (USITC) imposed ADD on shrimp imports from India and Thailand on the basis of the anti-dumping petition by Ad Hoc Shrimp Trade Action Committee (ASTAC), an association of shrimp farmers in eight southern states of the United States, although there was discussion on withdrawal/revision of this duty owing to the December 2004 tsunami disaster.[6] Bhattarcharyya (2006) noted that the Seafoods Exporters Association of India (SEAI) had tried to defend the cheaper price of Indian shrimp citing two major differences of the same with the US variety:

> First, there are specific variations between the shrimp caught off the south-west coast of the United States and in Indian waters, so that prices are bound to be different. "The threat for the domestic shrimp farmer in the United States comes from China, Thailand, Indonesia and Ecuador. India's shrimp exports are predominantly of black tiger and scampi varieties which are not cultivated in the United States", according to the president of SEAI.
>
> Second, while fishing in the United States is a capital-intensive activity calling for major investment, in India shrimp capture is carried out with a very low level of capital and requiring hardly any investment. This makes the cost of production considerably lower in India compared with that for shrimp sea-caught off the US coast.

In this background, India's negotiating strategy on anti-dumping at the WTO needs to be focused. The negotiating strategy of India has so far been a combination of defensive as well as proactive strategies, and stressed on ensuring special and differential treatment (SDT) for developing countries as well as revision of the ADA at the earliest. In the post-Doha period, India was focusing more on modification of the ADA for relaxing several provisions for developing countries, which is not the right approach. While revision of the floor levels, as depicted in the paragraphs below, does not provide a permanent solution, it technically acknowledges the possibility of dumping from developing countries (at least on some occasions)! There is no need to ask for SDT by the developing countries, the misuses of ADA by developed countries prepares a case strong enough to call for reform of the provision. India has raised the following points in the Doha Round on reforming the ADA:

---

6. US Government Document (2005).

- The existing *de minimis* dumping margin of 2 per cent of export price below which no anti-dumping duty can be imposed (Article 5.8), needs to be raised to 5 per cent for imports from developing countries.
- The threshold volume of dumped imports which shall normally be regarded as negligible (Article 5.8) should be increased from the existing 3 per cent to 5 per cent for imports from developing countries. Moreover, the stipulation that anti-dumping action can still be taken even if the volume of imports is below this threshold level, provided countries which individually account for less than the threshold volume, collectively account for more than 7 per cent of the imports, should be deleted.
- The lesser duty rule shall be made mandatory while imposing an anti-dumping duty against imports from developing-country Member by any developed-country Member.[7]

In the subsequent period, India modified its stance to some extent and asked for reform in Article 5.4 (lower limit on the proportion of domestic production affected by dumping), Article 2.2.2 (procedure for collecting cost and profit data), Article 2.4.2 (procedures for establishing margins of dumping), Article 3.4 (consideration of all relevant economic factors for examining the impact of dumping), Article 3.5 (demonstration of injury by dumped imports), Article 3.8 (application of anti-dumping measures with special care), Article 6.8 (final determination on the basis of 'available facts'), Article 11 (Duration and Review of Anti-dumping Duties and Price Undertakings) and finally Annex II (determination on the basis of best information available when collecting direct evidence is a problem).[8] The detailed proposals are shown in Annex A-8.1. The potential of applying WTO-incompatible policies in terms of these articles have already been mentioned earlier. However, the focus on availability of SDT for developing countries has been revisited at times. At the General Council session on 24 July 2003, India proposed a specific short-term dispensation in favour of developing countries in the form of a grace period of two years during which no anti-dumping investigations on imports of textile and clothing products from

7. India's submission to WTO, Document No. TN/RL/W/4 (Dated 25 April 2002).
8. India's submission to WTO, Document No. TN/RL/W/26 (Dated 17 October 2002).

developing countries shall be initiated.[9] Supporting this demand in the following period, India explained the massive impact of anti-dumping investigations on its domestic industries to the WTO:

> Reinforcing the protectionist motivation was also the fact that, in several instances, investigations into the same products were revived back-to-back, extending over long periods. In the case of one product (cotton fabrics), these were continued for five years. In the case of another (bed linen), these have been going on in one form or the other since January 1994.[10]

The Way Ahead

The messy state of affairs in this field has been best summarised by Messerlin (2001: 157), who notes, "There is no anti-dumping provision in GATS and—following the disastrous experience of anti-dumping in goods—one can only hope that there will never be." The validity of the statement can be best understood with respect to the summarised findings of select anti-dumping cases presented in Table 8.6. As already mentioned earlier, the increasing usage of this provision urged the members to place this concern at the Doha ministerial (2001), and subsequently the Doha Ministerial Declaration (paragraph 28) noted:

> In the light of experience and of the increasing application of these instruments by members, we agree to negotiations aimed at clarifying and improving disciplines under the Agreements on Implementation of Article VI of the GATT 1994 and on Subsidies and Countervailing Measures, while preserving the basic concepts, principles and effectiveness of these Agreements and their instruments and objectives, and taking into account the needs of developing and least-developed participants. In the initial phase of the negotiations, participants will indicate the provisions, including disciplines on trade distorting practices, that they seek to clarify and improve in the subsequent phase.

However, the discussions and negotiations failed to improve the scenario and the concerns were once again raised at the Cancun Ministerial (2003). The Cancun Ministerial Declaration (paragraph 7) noted that:

> We instruct the Negotiating Group on Rules to accelerate its work on anti-dumping and subsidies and countervailing measures, including fisheries subsidies, with a view to shifting its emphasis from identifying issues to seeking solutions.

---

9. "India seeks Transparency in the Cancun process", *India and the WTO*, Vol. 5, No. 6-7, p. 7, 2003.
10. India's submission to WTO, Document No. WT/GC/W/502 (Dated 14 July 2003).

Table 8.6

Select WTO Cases on Anti-Dumping Issues

Case No.	*Appellant*	*Respondent*	*Alleged Violation*	*WTO Ruling*
DS 295 (2003)	United States	Mexico	Certain provisions of Mexico's Foreign Trade Act and its Federal Code of Civil Procedure were inconsistent with – • Articles 5.8, 6, 6.1.1, 6.8, 7, 9, 9.5, 10.6, 11 and 11.1 of the ADA • Articles 11.9, 12.1.1, 12.7, 17, 19, 19.3, 20.6, 21 and 21.1 of the SCM	The Panel result is expected soon. (2003)
DS 277 (2003)	Canada	United States	US measures are inconsistent with - • Article VI:6(a) of the GATT 1994 • Articles 1, 3.1, 3.2, 3.3, 3.4, 3.5, 3.7, 3.8, 12 and 18.1 of the ADA • Articles 10, 15.1, 15.2, 15.3, 15.4, 15.5, 15.7, 15.8, 22 and 32.1 of the SCM	The Panel found that US acted inconsistently with – • Articles 3.5 and 3.7 the ADA • Article 15.5 and 15.7 of the SCM Agreement.
DS 268 (2002)	Argentina	United States	Final determinations of the US Department of Commerce are inconsistent with - • Articles 1, 2, 3, 5, 6, 11, 12, and 18 of the ADA • Articles VI and X of the GATT 1994 • Article XVI:4 of the WTO Agreement	The Panel concluded that the USDOC acted inconsistently with certain provisions of the ADA, but did not act inconsistently with other provisions of that Agreement.
DS 264 (2002)	Canada	United States	The determination under section 735 of the Tariff Act of 1930 is inconsistent with – • Articles 1, 2.1, 2.2, 2.4, 2.6, 5.1, 5.2, 5.3, 5.4, 5.8, 6.1, 6.2, 6.4, 6.9 and 9.3 of the ADA • Articles VI and X:3(a) of the GATT 1994	The Panel found that USDOC failed to comply with the requirements of Articles 2.4.2 of the AD Agreement. The Appellate Body upheld most of the findings and reversed some in Canada's favour.

contd. ...

... contd. ...

Case No.	Appellant	Respondent	Alleged Violation	WTO Ruling
DS 244 (2002)	Japan	United States	Sunset review of the anti-dumping duties on several commodities are inconsistent with – • Articles VI and X of GATT 1994 • Articles 2, 3, 5, 6 (including Annex II), 11, 12, and 18.4 of the ADA • Article XVI:4 of the WTO Agreement.	The Panel rejected all of Japan's claims challenging various aspects of the US laws and regulations regarding the conduct of 'sunset' reviews of anti-dumping duties under US law. Although the Appellate Body reversed four of the Panel's legal findings, they concluded that the US had acted WTO-consistently.
DS 241 (2001)	Brazil	Argentina	Articles 1, 2, 3, 4, 5, 6, 9, 12 and Annex II of the Anti-Dumping Agreement, Article VI of the GATT 1994, and Articles 1 and 7 of the Customs Valuation Agreement	The Panel found that Argentina had acted inconsistently with its obligations under Articles 2.4, 2.4.2, 3.1, 3.2, 3.3, 3.4, 3.5, 5.1, 5.8, 6.1.1, 6.1.3, 6.8 and Annex II, 6.10 and 12.1 of the Anti-Dumping Agreement.
DS 219 (2001)	Brazil	European Communities	EC had acted inconsistently with – • Article VI of GATT 1994 • Articles 1, 2, 3, 4 , 5, 6, 7, 9, 11, 12 and 15 of the ADA	The Panel concluded that the EC had acted inconsistently with Articles 2.4.2, 12.2 and 12.2.2 of the ADA. Although the Appellate Body rejected several claims made by Brazil, they concluded that EC acted inconsistently with Articles 6.2 and 6.4 of the ADA.
DS 211 (2000)	Turkey	Egypt	The Investigations by Egypt is inconsistent with – • Articles 2.2, 2.4, 3.1, 3.2, 3.4, 3.5, 6.1, 6.2, 6.6, 6.7 and 6.8, and Annex II, Paragraphs 1, 3, 5, 6 and 7 and Annex I, Paragraph 7 of the ADA • Article X:3 of the GATT 1994	Although the Panel rejected a number of claims made by Turkey, they found the Egyptian measure to be inconsistent with a number of WTO agreements.
DS 184 (1999)	Japan	United States	Certain provisions of the Tariff Act of 1930 and related regulations are inconsistent with– • Articles VI and X of the GATT 1994 • Articles 2, 3, 6 (including Annex II), 9 and 10 of the ADA	The Panel found that US acted inconsistently with Articles 2.1, 6.8, 9.4, 18.4 and Annex II of the ADA. The Appellate Body, however, reversed the Panel's findings on several points.

contd. ...

... *contd.* ...

Case No.	*Appellant*	*Respondent*	*Alleged Violation*	*WTO Ruling*
DS 179 (1999)	Korea	United States	US determination of Anti-Dumping Duty is inconsistent with – • Article VI of GATT 1994 • Articles 2, 6 and 12 of the ADA	Although the Panel rejected some of Korea's claims, it concluded that US acted inconsistently with Article 2.4 of ADA.
DS 162 (1999)	Japan	United States	The judicial decisions under the US 1916 Act are inconsistent with – • Articles III, VI and XI of GATT 1994 • Several provisions of ADA	The Panel concluded that the US has acted inconsistently with – • Article VI:1, VI:2 and XVI:4 of the GATT 1994 and • Article 1, 4.1, 5.1, 5.2, 5.4, 18.1 of the ADA The Appellate Body upheld all of the findings and conclusions of the panel.
DS 156 (1999)	Mexico	Guatemala	The definitive measure is inconsistent with – • Articles 1, 2, 3, 5, 6, 7, 12 and 18 of the ADA and its Annexes I and II • Article VI of GATT 1994	The alleged measure is inconsistent with Article 3.1, 3.2 3.4, 3.5, 5.3, 5.5, 5.8, 6.1.2, 6.1.3, 6.2, 6.4, 6.5, 6.8, 6.9, 12.1.1 and Annex I of the ADA.
DS 136 (1998)	European Communities	United States	The existence of 1916 Act in parallel with the Tariff Act of 1930 is inconsistent with – • Articles III:4, VI:1, and VI:2 of GATT 1994 • Article XVI:4 of the WTO Agreement • Articles 1, 2, 3, 4 and 5 of the ADA	The Panel concluded that the 1916 Act is inconsistent with – • Article VI:1 and VI:2 of the GATT 1994 • Articles 1, 4 and 5.5 of the ADA • Article XVI:4 of the WTO Agreement The Appellate Body upheld all of the findings and conclusions of the panel.
DS 132 (1998)	United States	Mexico	The Mexican measure is inconsistent with Articles 2, 3, 4, 5, 6, 7, 9, 10 and 12 of the ADA.	The alleged measure is inconsistent with Articles 3.1, 3.2, 3.4, 3.7 and 3.7(i), 5.2, 5.3, 5.8, 7.4, 10.2, 10.4, 12.1, 12.1.1(iv), 12.2 and 12.2.2 of the ADA.

contd. ...

... contd. ...

Case No.	*Appellant*	*Respondent*	*Alleged Violation*	*WTO Ruling*
DS 122 (1998)	Poland	Thailand	The imposition of final duties is inconsistent with Articles 2, 3, 5 and 6 of the ADA.	The Panel found that the measure is inconsistent with – • Articles 2 and 3 of the ADA • Article VI of the GATT 1994The Appellate Body upheld the major findings of the Panel.
DS 99 (1997)	Korea	United States	The anti-dumping duty on certain types of Dynamic Random Access Memory Semiconductors is inconsistent with Articles 6 and 11 of the ADA.	The Panel found the alleged measures is inconsistent with Article 11.2 of the ADA.
DS 60 (1996)	Mexico	Guatemala	The anti-dumping investigation is inconsistent with Articles 2, 3, 5 and 7.1 of the ADA.	The Panel found that the measure is inconsistent with Article 5.3 of the ADA. However, the Appellate Body reversed the Panel's finding that the dispute was properly before the Panel, as Mexico did not comply with Article 6.2 of the DSU in its request for a panel since it did not identify the measure it was complaining against, and could not make any conclusions on the findings by the Panel.

Source: WTO Documents.

Following the heavy criticism on the Derbez draft, negotiations were stalled, and when resumed again in July 2004, the anti-dumping provision was clearly not the focus of the meeting. The Hong Kong Ministerial declaration (2005) took note of the concerns and the state of negotiations and for the first time anti-dumping provisions have been mentioned separately in an annex (Annex D.I on rules), as mentioned in the following:

- "*Consider* that negotiations on anti-dumping should, as appropriate, clarify and improve the rules regarding, *inter alia*, (a) determinations of dumping, injury and causation, and the application of measures; (b) procedures governing the initiation, conduct and completion of anti-dumping investigations, including with a view to strengthening due process and enhancing transparency; and (c) the level, scope and duration of measures, including duty assessment, interim and new shipper reviews, sunset, and anti-circumvention proceedings;
- *Recognise* that negotiations on anti-dumping have intensified and deepened, that Participants are showing a high level of constructive engagement, and that the process of rigorous discussion of the issues based on specific textual proposals for amendment to the AD Agreement has been productive and is a necessary step in achieving the substantial results to which Ministers are committed;
- *Note* that, in the negotiations on anti-dumping, the Negotiating Group on Rules has been discussing in detail proposals on such issues as determinations of injury/causation, the lesser duty rule, public interest, transparency and due process, interim reviews, sunset, duty assessment, circumvention, the use of facts available, limited examination and all others rates, dispute settlement, the definition of dumped imports, affiliated parties, product under consideration, and the initiation and completion of investigations, and that this process of discussing proposals before the Group or yet to be submitted will continue after Hong Kong."

Given the experience on anti-dumping investigations, there is an urgent need to look into the modification of the procedure, and the current analysis attempts to identify the potential candidates for future reform. It seems from the massive violations in the ADA that in future the continuation of the mechanism itself should be questioned. However, it is unlikely, at least as of now, that the members would agree to get rid of this entire mechanism. Therefore, the focus of the future negotiations should be on reform of those articles of ADA, which leave room for various interpretations for fulfilling protectionist purposes, and on limiting the use of the very mechanism itself. The identified 'misused' articles in Figure 8.2 are strong candidates for that purpose. Last but not the least, tackling the increasing trend of anti-dumping investigations in the developing countries should be a priority area, since the consumers in those locations get affected much more severely than their counterparts in developed countries in the entire process.

References

Aggarwal, Aradhna (2004). "Developing Countries and the WTO Anti-dumping Code: Issues and Suggestions", in Bibek Debroy and Mohd. Saqib (eds.), *Future Negotiation Issues at WTO: An India-China Perspective*, pp. 345-377, Globus Books, New Delhi.

Almstedt, Kermit and Norton Patrick (2000). "China's Anti-dumping Laws and WTO Anti-dumping Agreement", (Including Comments on Chain's Early Enforcement of its Anti-dumping Laws), *Journal of World Trade*, 34(6), pp. 75-113.

Banik, Nilanjan (1998). "Anti-Dumping Measures—An Indian Perspective", *RGICS Working Paper* Series, No. 1, Rajiv Gandhi Institute for Contemporary Studies, New Delhi.

Bhattarcharyya, B. (2006). "The Indian Shrimp Industry Organises to Fight the Threat of Anti-Dumping Action", Managing the Challenges of WTO Participation: Case Study 17, World Trade Organization, available at *http://www.wto.org/english/res_e/booksp_e/casestudies_e/case17_e.htm*.

Chakraborty, Debashis and Julien Chaisse (2005). "Trade Policy Review Mechanism and Dispute Settlement System: A Cross-Country Analysis of Enforcing WTO Rules between Negotiations and Sanctions", in Bibek Debroy and Md. Saqib (eds.), *WTO at Ten: Looking Back to Look Beyond*, pp. 210-278, Konark Publishers, New Delhi.

Debroy, Bibek and Nilanjan Banik (2000). "The Dumping Issue", *Global Business Review*, 1(1), pp. 75-90.

Economic and Social Commission for Asia and the Pacific (2000). "Non-tariff Measures with Potentially Restrictive Market Access Implications Emerging in a Post-Uruguay Round Context", *Studies in Trade and Investment*, No. 40, United Nations, New York.

Government of India (various issues). *India and the WTO*, The monthly Newsletter of Ministry of Commerce, Ministry of Commerce, New Delhi.

———. (2004). "Annual Report of Directorate General of Anti-Dumping and Allied Duties—2003-04", Ministry of Commerce, New Delhi.

———. (2003). "Anti-dumping Actions in the Area of Textiles and Clothing: Proposal for a Specific Short-Term Dispensation in Favour of Developing Members Following Full Integration of the Sector into GATT 1994 from January 2005", Submitted by India, WTO Document No. WT/GC/W/502 (Dated 14 July).

———. (2002a). "Proposals on Anti-Dumping Agreement", Submitted by India, WTO Document No. TN/RL/W/26 (Dated 17 October).

———. (2002b). "Proposals on Implementation related Issues and Concerns", Submitted by India, WTO Document No. TN/RL/W/4 (Dated 25 April).

Irwin, Douglas A. (2002). "Free Trade under Fire", Princeton University Press, Princeton, New Jersey.

Khan, Amir Ullah (2001). "Dumping Procedures: Looking Into the Issues", in the seminar on *The New WTO Round: Is Free Trade Fair Trade?*, jointly organised by Rajiv Gandhi Institute for Contemporary Studies and Liberty Institute, October 12, New Delhi.

Lindsey, Brink and Daniel Ikenson (2002). "Reforming the Anti-dumping Agreement: A Road Map for WTO Negotiations", *Trade Policy Analysis* No. 21, Cato Institute, Washington DC.

Messerlin, Patrick A. (2001). "Anti-Dumping and Trade Remedies: A Necessary Reform", in Klaus Gunter Deutsch and Bernhard Speyer (eds.), *The World Trade Organization Millennium Round: Freer Trade in the Twenty-First Century*, pp. 148-160, Routledge, London and New York.

Raju, K.D. (2004). "Future of Anti-dumping: Call for Reform", in the Conference on *Looking Beyond Cancun: The Trend in Trade Talk*, organised by Rajiv Gandhi Institute for Contemporary Studies and Liberty Institute, March 24, New Delhi.

MVIRDC (1994). "GATT Agreements: Final Text of Uruguay Round", World Trade Centre, Mumbai.

United States Trade Representative, Government of US (2006). "Foreign Trade Barriers", *India*, pp. 300-14.

———. (2005). "Dumping Duties on Shrimp from India, Thailand Under Review", April 25, *http://canberra.usembassy.gov/hyper/2005/0425/epf103.htm.*

World Trade Organization "WTO Annual Report", (Various issues), WTO, Geneva.

———. (1998). "India", *Trade Policy Review*, WTO, Geneva.

———. (2002). "India", *Trade Policy Review*, WTO, Geneva.

———. (2005). "Update of WTO Dispute Settlement Cases", *WTO Document No.* WT/DS/OV/23 (Dated 7 April, 2005), WTO, Geneva.

Annexure A-8.1

India's Submission to WTO on Anti-Dumping Agreement (Document No. TN/RL/W/26, Dated 17 October 2002)

- *Back to back anti-dumping investigation:* A new paragraph Article 5.4 *bis* may be inserted requiring that an investigating authority shall not initiate an anti-dumping investigation where an investigation on the same product or a broader category of another product which included the product now under consideration from the same member resulted in negative finding within 365 days prior to the filing of the petition seeking initiation of a new investigation.
- *Domestic industry consisting of small-scale or 'unorganised' sector producers:* The Anti-Dumping Agreement must be amended to clarify that footnote 13 also applies to the 25 per cent requirement in the last sentence of Article 5.4.
- *Article 2.2.2—Hierarchy of options:* It is therefore proposed that an amendment be carried out in the chapters of Article 2.2.2 specifying that the three options thereunder have a hierarchical significance and a subsequent option may be resorted to only in the absence of relevant data under the preceding option(s).
- *Application of a Reasonability Test under Article 2.2:* In order to ensure the reasonableness of amount of profit under options 2.2.2(i) and 2.2.2(ii) the limitation enshrined in option 2.2.2(iii) i.e. the profit to be reasonable and should not exceed profit normally realised by other exporters or producers on sales of same product or the same general category of products, as appropriate could be imposed.
- *Prohibition on zeroing of dumping margins:* There should be an explicit clarification in Article 2.4.2 prohibiting those comparisons between export price and normal value that do not fully take into account the prices of all comparable export transactions such as the practice of zeroing while establishing the margins of dumping on the basis of comparison of a weighted average normal value with a weighted average prices of all export transactions.
- *Rules for determination of injury margin shall be introduced:* A variety of questions were raised relating to 'objectivity' and 'transparency' in calculation of injury margins, selection of 'domestic producers', time period for injury, the appropriate occasion for using 'price under-cutting/price under-selling', adjustments between the 'landed price and the domestic sales price' and determination of 'dumping margins'.
- *Elaboration of injury factors referred to in Article 3.4:* Some of the mandatory injury parameters require further elaboration for ensuring consistency and predictability among investigating authorities while making an assessment of the consequent impact of dumped imports on the domestic products of the like product.
- *'Non-attribution clause' i.e. for segregating injury caused by factors other than dumped imports referred to in Article 3.5 shall be elaborated:* It is essential to elaborate Article 3.5 so that appropriate guidance is provided to investigating authorities while separating and distinguishing the injurious effects of other factors from the injurious effects caused by the dumped imports. Furthermore, to invoke anti-dumping measures, there is a need to specify an

appropriate standard for establishing causality between dumped imports and material injury.

- *'Special care' requirement in respect of determination of threat of material injury referred to in Article 3.8 shall be elaborated:* It is proposed that 'special care' needs an elaboration so that a clear, specific and unambiguous benchmark is specified.
- *Price Undertakings:* A variety of questions were raised relating to 'determine price undertaking', 'satisfactory' and 'unsatisfactory' price undertakings, conditions for non-acceptance of price undertakings.
- *Rules relating to reviews:* A new provision needs to be added to Article 11 whereby a review can be undertaken on the basis of positive evidence submitted by any interested party based on the findings of the judicial review establishing that the underlying investigation was flawed.
- *Concurrent application of anti-dumping and safeguard measures:* In situations which result in concurrent imposition of anti-dumping and safeguard measures on the same product the imposition of anti-dumping measure shall be suspended or the level of duty adjusted as long as the safeguard measure is enforced.
- *Clarification in respect of resort to facts available under Article 6.8 and Annex II of the Anti-Dumping Agreement:* There should be clear guidance specifying the circumstances in which an investigating authority may resort to total facts available. In other situations the investigating authority shall be required to take into consideration all information which meets the criteria of Annex II:3, although some other information may not meet this criteria.

ANNEXURE

Differential and More Favourable Treatment for Developing and Least Developed Countries in Various WTO Agreements

Concerns Regarding Implementation—Anti-Dumping Measures
(The Indian View)

" ... we find that anti-dumping measures are being virtually used as weapons by certain developed countries to deny access to the products of developing countries. On the same commodity, anti-dumping action has been repeatedly initiated by certain developed countries. This has created instability and unpredictability in the market, which militates against basic GATT principles. It is vitally important to lay down clear guidelines for making sure that the provision in Article 15 is translated into practice. Some areas where special and differential treatment can be considered for exports from developing country members are enumerated below:

a) A *de minimis* dumping margin limit of 2 per cent of export price has been prescribed and no anti-dumping duty can be imposed if the dumping margin is below this threshold limit. This *de minimis* limit is the same for exports from developing as well as from developed countries. Many of the export products of developing countries are produced by labour intensive small and medium enterprises. Imposition of anti-dumping duties, or even the threat of imposition of such duties has a serious adverse effect on the functioning of such units. As a consequence, there is fall in production, heavy unemployment, decline in incomes and increase in poverty levels. In view of the high sensitivity of these sectors to any export disruption, the *de minimis* dumping margin of 2 per cent should be enhanced. The level of enhancement in respect of each developing and least developed country should reflect the disadvantage that the industry in such country suffers *vis-à-vis* comparable production in developed countries. For instance, the Federation of Indian Chambers of Commerce and Industry has estimated that the disadvantage suffered by Indian industry by way of differential costs of working capital, financing cost of refund of excise duty, intangible infrastructure costs, sales tax on local bought outs and octroi amounts to approximately 17 per cent. The inherently high prices sometimes maintainable in the domestic market are not sustainable in exports, and the prices of the latter often represent reduced levels of profitability for the exporters. The price differential of 2 per cent presently constituting the *de minimis* dumping margin is unrealistically low. However, the extent of disadvantage would vary from country to country and its assessment could be a cumbersome, contentious issue. Hence, it is better to have an across-the-board *de minimis* which could be prescribed *vis-à-vis* all developing countries to adequately reflect the higher price levels which prevail in such countries.

b) Article 5.8 of the Anti-Dumping Agreement presently provides that the volume of dumped imports shall normally be regarded as negligible, if the volume of dumped imports from a particular country is found to account for less than 3 per cent of imports of the like product, unless countries which individually account for less than 3 per cent of the imports of the like product collectively account for more than 7 per cent of the imports into the importing Members. In view of the liberalisation of global trade and in view of the fact that more and more developing countries are entering into what were earlier untapped markets for them; it is necessary to increase these percentages with a view to help developing countries. These percentages should be increased respectively to 7 per cent and 15 per cent in the case of imports from a developing country into a developed country.

c) Since, anti-dumping investigations are against specific exporters, the impact of investigations and the resulting duties, if any, are felt by the exporters from developing countries who, more often than not, are very small in size and operations. The cost of defending the interests of the exporters of the developing country Members is also prohibitive and a matter of concern. It is, therefore, important and that investigations should be initiated against developing country members only if the petition has the support of at least 50 per cent of the domestic industry of the developed country Members. Further, no investigation should be initiated for a period of 365 days from the date of finalisation of previous investigation for the same product resulting in non-imposition of duties. However, if it is established by the complainants that the circumstances have changed drastically subsequently to the finalisation of a case, such investigation should be initiated only if it has the support of at least 75 per cent of the domestic industry of the developed country Members.

Further, stricter criteria should be applied for such repeated investigation and this should not be less than one year. Guidelines should be established to define the parameters of establishing 'drastic' change of circumstances and the 'stricter criteria' to be applied in such cases.

d) Article 9.1 of the Agreement allows the investigating authorities to impose anti-dumping duties where all requirements for imposition have been fulfilled. This Article further states that it is desirable that the duty be less than the margin of dumping if such lesser duty would be adequate to remove the injury to the domestic industry. It is matter of concern that a large number of developed countries, who also happen to be active users of the mechanism, apply duties to the full extent of the margin of dumping. While the Agreement does not make it obligatory for the investigating authorities to follow the 'lesser duty rule' the application of duties to the full extent of dumping margins invariably leads to higher level of protection to the domestic industry, which is in excess of the duty required to negate the injury caused to their domestic industry. It would be appropriate, therefore, to have a special provision that the application of the lesser duty rule be made mandatory when a developed country member is investigating the alleged dumped imports from a developing country member. In addition, norms and criteria should be established to operationalise the 'lesser duty' route in terms of 'adequacy' to remove 'injury'.

e) The Agreement of Anti-Dumping has severely limited the role of panels in disputes relating to Anti-Dumping. Article 17.6 lays down that if the panel finds that the authorities have established and evaluated facts properly, objectively and without bias, it shall not overturn the conclusion reached by the authorities even though, on the basis of same facts, the panel itself would have decided differently. Since, developed countries are increasingly resorting to the use of anti-dumping duties against developing countries, it is necessary that what is applicable to disputes relating to other covered agreements is made applicable to disputes relating to anti-dumping."

Source: *India and the WTO*, Vol. 1, No. 4, April 1999.

Index

B

D

E

F

J

K

L

M

N

O

P

LIBERTY

Liberty Institute

Liberty Institute is an independent think tank dedicated to empowering the people by harnessing the power of the market. It seeks to build understanding and appreciation of the four institutional pillars of a free society — *Individual Rights, Rule of Law, Limited Government* and *Free Market*.

The Institute undertakes a number of activities, among them research and advocacy on public policy issues. It organises conferences, and has a growing publications programme. At present, the Institute's core areas of interest include development economics, education, environment, health, security, and trade.

The Institute was established in 1996 as a non-profit organisation. It solicits the support of all freedom loving individuals and organisations. It strives to retain its independence, demonstrate its commitment, and live up to its motto: *"Where the mind is without fear…"*

LIBERTY INSTITUTE
Julian L. Simon Centre, C-4/8, Sahyadri, Plot 5, Sector 12, Dwarka, Phase I, New Delhi 110 075. India
Tel: 91-11-25079215. Fax: 91-11-25079101. Email: info@libertyindia.org, liberty@nda.vsnl.net.in
Websites: www.libertyindia.org